Conservative Moments

TEXTUAL MOMENTS IN THE HISTORY OF POLITICAL THOUGHT

Series Editor

J. C. Davis, Emeritus Professor of History,
University of East Anglia, UK
John Morrow, Professor of Political Studies,
University of Auckland, New Zealand

Textual Moments provides accessible, short readings of key texts in selected fields of political thought, encouraging close reading informed by cutting-edge scholarship. The unique short essay format of the series ensures that volumes cover a range of texts in roughly chronological order. The essays in each volume aim to open up a reading of the text and its significance in the political discourse in question and in the history of political thought more widely. Key moments in the textual history of a particular genre of political discourse are made accessible, appealing and instructive to students, scholars and general readers.

Published

Censorship Moments: Reading Texts in the History of Censorship and Freedom of Expression, Geoff Kemp
Democratic Moments, Xavier Márquez
Feminist Moments: Reading Feminist Texts, Susan Bruce and Katherine Smits
Liberal Moments: Reading Liberal Texts, Ewa Atanassow and Alan S. Kahan
Patriarchal Moments: Reading Patriarchal Texts, Cesare Cuttica and Gaby Mahlberg
Revolutionary Moments: Reading Revolutionary Texts, Rachel Hammersley
Utopian Moments: Reading Utopian Texts, Miguel Avilés and J. C. Davis

Conservative Moments

Reading Conservative Texts

EDITED BY
MARK GARNETT

BLOOMSBURY ACADEMIC
LONDON • NEW YORK • OXFORD • NEW DELHI • SYDNEY

BLOOMSBURY ACADEMIC
Bloomsbury Publishing Plc
50 Bedford Square, London, WC1B 3DP, UK

BLOOMSBURY, BLOOMSBURY ACADEMIC and the Diana logo are trademarks of
Bloomsbury Publishing Plc

First published in Great Britain 2018

A catalogue record for this book is available from the British Library.

A catalog record for this book is available from the Library of Congress.

ISBN: HB: 978-1-3500-0153-4
PB: 978-1-3500-0152-7
ePDF: 978-1-3500-0155-8
eBook: 978-1-3500-0154-1

Series: Textual Moments in the History of Political Thought

Typeset by Newgen KnowledgeWorks Pvt. Ltd., Chennai, India

To find out more about our authors and books visit www.bloomsbury.com
and sign up for our newsletters.

CONTENTS

NOTES ON CONTRIBUTORS

David S. Bell is emeritus professor of French Government and Politics in the University of Leeds. His books include *Parties and Democracy in France: Parties under Presidentialism* (2010) and *François Mitterand: A Political Biography* (2005).

Elena Chebankova is a reader in the School of Social and Political Sciences, University of Lincoln. She has published numerous articles on ideology in Russia, and her books include *Civil Society in Putin's Russia* (2015).

Wendell John Coats is professor of Government at Connecticut College. He is the author of several books, including *Oakeshott and His Contemporaries* (2000), *Political Theory and Practice* (2003) and *Montaigne's Essais* (2004).

Donald T. Critchlow is professor of history at Arizona State University. He has written many books and articles on various aspects on US political history, including *The Conservative Ascendancy: How the GOP Right Made Political History* (2007), and *Future Right: Forging a New Republican Majority* (2016).

Joseph Ellis is an associate professor of political science at Wingate University. He has published several articles on politics in Eastern Europe.

Michael Federici is professor of political science at Mercyhurst University and director of the National Humanities Institute's Center for Constitutional Studies. He is the author of numerous books and articles, including *The Challenge of Populism: The Rise of Right-Wing Democratism in Postwar America* (1991), and *The Political Philosophy of Alexander Hamilton* (2012).

Allen James Fromherz is the director of Middle East Studies at Georgia State University. Among numerous books and articles, he is the author of *Ibn Khaldun: Life and Times* (2010) and *The Almohads: The Rise of an Islamic Empire* (2010).

Mark Garnett is a senior lecturer in Politics and International Relations at Lancaster University. He has published many books and articles on post-war British Politics, including *Principles and Politics in Contemporary Britain* (2006) and (with Kevin Hickson) *Conservative Thinkers: The Key Contributors to the Political Thought of the Modern Conservative Party* (2009).

James Harris is professor of the History of Philosophy at the University of St Andrews. Among many publications, he is the author of *Hume: An Intellectual Biography* (2015), and the editor of *The Oxford Handbook of British Philosophy in the Eighteenth Century* (2013).

Simon Mabon is a lecturer in Politics and International Relations at Lancaster University, and director of the Richardson Institute for Peace Studies. Among numerous publications, he is the author of *Saudi Arabia and Iran: Power and Rivalry in the Middle East* (2015), and (with Stephen Royle) *The Origins of ISIS: The Collapse of Nations and Revolution in the Middle East* (2015).

John Morrow is professor of Political Studies and deputy vice-chancellor (Academic) at the University of Auckland, New Zealand. His publications include *Coleridge's Political Thought* (1990) (with Mark Francis), *A History of Nineteenth-Century English Political Thought* (1994) and *The History of Political Thought: A Thematic Introduction* (1998).

Kieron O'Hara is an associate professor and principal research fellow in the Department of Electronics and Computer Science in the University of Southampton. Among his numerous publications are *After Blair: Conservatism beyond Thatcher* (2005), and *Conservatism* (2011).

Efraim Podoksik is a senior lecturer in political science at the Hebrew University of Jerusalem. He is the editor of *The Cambridge Companion to Oakeshott* (2011), and author of *In Defence of Modernity: The Social Thought of Michael Oakeshott* (2003), among many books and articles.

Casey Pratt is an associate professor and the English and Education Programme coordinator for the Department of English and Modern Languages, Wingate University.

David Lewis Schaefer is professor of Political Theory at the College of the Holy Cross. Among many books and articles, he is the author of *The Political Philosophy of Montaigne* (1990) and *Illiberal Justice: John Rawls vs. The American Political Tradition* (2007).

Martin Steven is a lecturer in Politics and International Relations at Lancaster University. He has published numerous articles on European Politics, with particular emphasis on the role of religion, and is the author of *Christianity and Party Politics: Keeping the Faith* (2011).

Bekir Varoglu is a doctoral candidate at Lancaster University, researching ideology in contemporary Turkey.

Christian P. Winkler is a lecturer in Japanese Politics at Hokkaido University. He has written many articles on ideology in post-war Japan, and is the author of *The Quest for Japan's New Constitution: An Analysis of Visions and Constitutional Reform Proposals* (2010).

SERIES EDITORS' FOREWORD

At the heart of the serious study of the history of political thought, as expressed through both canonical and non-canonical works of all kinds, has been the question (to which we all too readily assume an answer), 'How shall I read this text?' Answers have varied greatly over time. Once the political works of the past – especially those of Classical Greece and Rome – were read with an eye to their immediate application to the present. And, until comparatively recently, the canonical works of political philosophy were selected and read as expressions of perennial, abiding truths about politics, social morality and justice. The problem was that this approach made little or no concession to historically changing contexts, that the 'truths' we identified were all too often *our* truths. A marxisant sociology of knowledge struggled to break free from the 'eternal verities' of political thought by exploring the ways in which past societies shaped their own forms of political expression in distinctive yet commonly grounded conceptions of their own image. The problem remained that the perception of what shaped past societies was all too often driven by the demands of a current political agenda. In both cases, present concerns shaped the narrative history of political thought off which the reading of texts fed. The last half century has seen another powerful and influential attempt to break free from a present-centred history of political thought by locating texts as speech acts or moves within a contemporary context of linguistic usage. Here the frequently perceived problem has been (a by-no-means inevitable) narrowing of focus to canonical texts, while the study of other forms of political expression in images, speech, performance and gesture – in all forms of political culture – has burgeoned independently.

We have, then, a variety of ways of approaching past texts and the interplay of text and context. The series 'Textual Moments in the History of Political Thought' (in which *Conservative Moments* is the eighth title) is designed to encourage fresh readings of thematically selected texts. Each chapter identifies a key textual moment or passage and exposes it to a reading by an acknowledged expert. The aim is fresh insight, accessibility, and the encouragement to read, in a more informed way for oneself.

Although conservative political movements have had a major impact in the modern world, and conservative ways of thinking have a long pedigree across the course of human history, conservative political thought has not been a major focus of academic writing. Even so, discussions of conservative ideas across time have been particularly bedeviled by definitional uncertainties, epitomized by Michael Oakeshott's suggestion that conservatism is best viewed as a psychological state rather than an ideology. This characterization would sit well with Oakeshott himself and with at least one of the other figures considered in this volume (David Hume) but is perhaps ill-suited to the highly volatile Edmund Burke, who is often regarded as a quintessentially conservative thinker, or the intensely combative Margaret Thatcher. In response to these definitional complexities, the editor of this volume adopts a working characterization of conservative thought which reflects the reaction (against a particular kind of rationalism) which distinguished the conservatism of Burke and some other contemporaneous commentators on the French Revolution: It is marked by 'an aversion towards radical change reflecting a belief in the imperfection of human nature'. Even so the diversity of directions taken by that reaction, from the insistence on pragmatism as vital to 'practical politics' to various ideologies resistant to radical change, remains a feature of twenty-first-century conservatism.

The essays that make up this volume demonstrate both the temporal and cultural range of conservative thinking. They draw on Western political thinking, and the early modern Islamic tradition, represented here by Ibn Khaldun, and consider conservative ideas in Russian, Turkish, German and Japanese contexts. Conservatives' stress on the practical and atheoretical character of their doctrine is reflected in the final set of essays which take statements from conservative politicians as starting points for considering the relationship between this way of thinking and political practice in the post-war world.

J. C. Davis
John Morrow

ACKNOWLEDGEMENTS

I am most grateful for the patience and support of Emily Drewe and Beatriz Lopez at Bloomsbury. The series editors John Morrow and Colin Davis have been meticulous in their oversight and have always been ready with constructive advice. Brian Garvey, my colleague in the Department of Politics, Philosophy and Religion at Lancaster, rode to the rescue when I was faced with some vexing technical matters. My chief debt, naturally, is to the contributors to this volume, whose work has deepened my own understanding of the subject.

INTRODUCTION

Mark Garnett

In a vivid phrase, the editors of another volume in this series have observed that 'To write about a tradition of political thought as rich as liberalism is something like trying to carry water in a leaky bucket.'[1] While conceding the difficulty of encapsulating the complexity of the liberal tradition in an edited collection of this nature, anyone undertaking the same task in relation to conservatism can (hopefully) be forgiven for feeling a twinge of envy. A bucket of any kind would be a luxury: compared to the liberal tradition, conservatism seems more like a sieve.

It would not be too difficult to track down two or more academic commentators who have broadly similar understandings of the nature of conservatism. However, this level of agreement is most commonly found among those who are openly *hostile* towards the conservative tradition. More sympathetic observers will usually find ample grounds for disagreement. Indeed, it is not uncommon to encounter the view that the hunt for any distinctive conservative 'tradition' will prove fruitless. Michael Oakeshott was not alone in eschewing the idea that conservatism could be classed as an approach to governance which could be considered to share key characteristics with socialism, liberalism, and the rest. 'Being Conservative', in Oakeshott's view, denoted a psychological state – a 'disposition' – rather than adherence to political ideas which could be boiled down into a set of precepts. Oakeshott's 'Conservative' turns out to be an individual who is far too balanced to take an obsessive interest in politics. As the mischievous Oakeshott probably realized, he was setting a standard which would deny the label of 'Conservative' to the overwhelming majority of British politicians and political theorists since the word started to be used in the early nineteenth century. Certainly on Oakeshott's evaluation, the great Liberal Party leader, Gladstone, who indulged in the non-political pastimes of chopping down trees and rescuing 'fallen women', exhibited more 'conservative' characteristics than his Conservative rival, Disraeli, whose extracurricular activities consisted chiefly of writing novels – about politics.

It could be argued that it would be easier to supply a satisfactory definition of conservatism if the subject had attracted more scholarly attention. More likely, there would have been a larger number of individuals expressing disagreement, or talking at cross-purposes. Nevertheless, it certainly is the case that, particularly in the English-speaking world, conservatism has not been studied as much as one might reasonably expect, given the success of political movements which, rightly or wrongly, are designated as being 'conservative' in nature. John Stuart Mill thought it 'obvious and undeniable' that, even if Conservatives were not generally stupid, 'stupid persons are generally Conservative'. Maybe Mill was right, and conservatism is just intellectually unrewarding. But, in addition, many open-minded academics have regarded conservatism as antipathetic to their vocation. If the greatest wisdom lies in recognition of the value of things as they are, for all their imperfections, why should anyone develop his or her own critical faculties, or help youthful minds to become more questioning? Others, undoubtedly, simply support political parties which are strongly opposed to rivals who either accept the 'conservative' label or have it imposed on them. From this perspective, all too often, attempts to understand the nature of conservatism are equated with unthinking opposition to people who want to change the world for the better.

Whatever the reasons for relative scholarly neglect, the result has been a host of questions about conservatism which are more often addressed by critics than by those who wish to provide plausible answers. For example, is conservatism inherently authoritarian? Does it lend itself to populist politics (epitomized by the 'Tea Party' movement in the United States and the subsequent phenomenon of a Trump presidency)? Is it reasonable to equate conservatives with 'reactionaries', who seek to restore an illusory golden age? To what extent does conservatism depend on religious faith? Does it foster a pugnacious brand of nationalism? Not least, can it be characterized as a more or less cynical attempt to justify inequalities of various kinds? – or do conservatives, rightly understood, regard inequality as an inescapable facet of the human condition?[2]

Perhaps the most intractable question relating to conservatism is whether it can be understood as a specific approach to politics, regardless of differences of time or place, or whether its meaning is context dependent? In other words, does 'conservatism' have an unchanging 'essence', or can it be susceptible to different interpretations depending on circumstances? The problem with the 'elastic' approach to 'conservatism' is that it reduces the value of the term as a tool of ideological analysis. At its least enlightening it can lead to apparent absurdities like the tendency in the 1980s to use the same word, 'conservative', in relation to free-market enthusiasts in the United States and the United Kingdom and the inflexible advocates of state control in the Soviet Union. Admittedly, this kind of muddle is more typical of media commentary than of academic analysis, but it undoubtedly affects the latter to some extent. Thus, for example, Leo Strauss (see Chapter 8) was educated in Europe, but his influence has been more significant in the United States. Strauss's main intellectual purpose was to disclose the intentions of the authors of classical texts in political thought. However, he did draw a clear distinction between liberalism and conservatism, and it is evident that he was strongly antipathetic to the former. Even quite well-informed observers might not be surprised, on this basis, to learn that Strauss is sometimes identified as the spiritual founder of 'neo-conservatism' in the United States. However, the neo-conservatives under President George W. Bush favoured an ideological crusade on behalf of liberal democracy – an initiative which would have horrified Strauss. The main problem, one could argue, is that Strauss's message was misunderstood by some of his self-styled disciples; but if some basic principles of conservatism could be agreed, there would be a much better chance of avoiding the kind of terminological confusion which presents opponents of liberalism as the inspiration for a group of neo-conservatives who were really radical liberals!

If dictionary definitions could resolve conflicts over the meaning of political labels, there would be no dispute about at least one feature of conservatism. The adjective 'conservative' denotes a desire to preserve existing conditions. It was first imported to the political context when the French writer François-René de Chateaubriand (1768–1848) founded the journal *Le Conservateur* in 1818. This provenance is not particularly helpful to an understanding of the ideology, since Chateaubriand's views oscillated between 'reactionary' support for a return to the pre-Revolutionary monarchical regime, and a much more liberal outlook, particularly on issues like freedom of speech.

There is a much better case for identifying an earlier writer, Edmund Burke (1729–97), as the 'founder' of modern conservatism (see Chapter 5). Burke's *Reflections on the Revolution in France* (1790) was not an attempt to turn back the clock, since it was composed before the French monarchy was overthrown. Rather, it could be read as an attempt to explain why the clock should be stopped from ticking. But even if Burke invited this interpretation by extolling the virtues of the French royal family – and seeming to favour a 'reactionary' turn, by evoking the far-distant 'age of chivalry' and convincing himself that life was good in mediaeval times – his tract included a defence of moderate reform, which was actually more consistent with his own activities as a middle-ranking politician.

As a playbook for politicians in late-eighteenth-century Europe (rather than a mere quarry of sparkling quotations) Burke's *Reflections* can be distilled into the advice that although 'existing conditions' were unlikely to be perfect, any attempt to remedy them through radical measures was likely to end in something far worse than the original disease. This was because, contrary to the assumptions of French Revolutionary ideologues, human beings were creatures of emotion rather than reason, and this was most unlikely to change. This claim about the human condition was certainly not original to Burke – it could be detected at least as far back as Plato (see Chapter 1), more than three centuries before the birth of Christ. Despite the very different context, Plato had wrestled with the questions that interested Burke, and from a broadly similar perspective – they shared an assumption that the 'average' human being was not equipped for rational decision-making on issues which concerned the community as a whole, and a corresponding concern that, in the interests of stability, political decisions should be left to those who were able to exercise considered judgement.

On this basis, we have a licence to carry our search for 'conservative moments' far beyond the controversy over the French Revolution, even if this condemns us to using a sieve rather than a leaky bucket. If conservatism can be defined very broadly as an aversion towards radical change, reflecting a belief in the imperfection of human nature, it could be identified across geographical as well as historical boundaries. Thus, the quest for 'early' conservative moments can encompass the Christian theologian St Augustine of Hippo (354–430) as well as the Islamic scholar and politician Ibn Khaldun (1332–1406: see Chapters 2 and 3). Augustine's *The City of God against the Pagans* provides an answer of sorts to Plato; while the latter envisaged a solution to political problems in a 'utopian' state governed by experts who had been trained from birth to overlook any personal interests, Augustine enjoined his readers to accept the imperfections of life on earth in the expectation of better things to come. Despite his piety, Ibn Khaldun took a keen interest in worldly matters – indeed, in the range of his intellectual achievements he is reminiscent of Aristotle, while his political insights, as both an observer and a practitioner, anticipate Machiavelli. While his thought is particularly difficult to categorize in ideological terms, his focus on the disruptive effects on social solidarity of luxury, greed and urban living in general makes it profitable to examine his thought in a volume on conservatism.

It could be suggested that these early writers contributed some fertile hints rather than self-conscious 'conservative moments'; and this remark could also be applied to David Hume (1771–76), who has often been characterized as a conservative but who did not live to witness the French Revolution, which polarized opinions in Europe. Hume did comment on the early stages of the American Revolutionary War (1775–83; see Chapter 4), in a way which provides suggestive comparisons with the reaction of Edmund Burke (who was sympathetic enough to make some observers believe that he would be equally supportive of subsequent developments in France). Certainly, if one accepts Oakeshott's notion that 'being Conservative' is related to an individual's 'dispostion', the amiable Hume was a far better example than the volcanic Burke. Hume's view that 'Reason is, and ought only to be the slave of the passions' can be compared to Burke's defence of 'prejudice' as a motive for action.

Hume's writings were well known to key figures in the early history of the American Republic, such as James Madison and Alexander Hamilton (1775–1804). The latter's ideological identity – like that of Hume himself – is warmly contested (see Chapter 6). However, the case for regarding Hamilton as a conservative seems particularly strong. After all, he was a direct participant in debates concerning the best form of government for his own country, while Burke was reflecting on developments in a neighbouring state, of which he had imperfect knowledge. In addition, Burke's main purpose was to reassert a 'conservative' reading of the political upheavals which had affected Britain in the seventeenth century, against radicals who argued that those events were merely the first instalment in an unfinished campaign to transform Britain's monarchical system into a 'rational' republic. In contrast, once the American colonies rejected British rule, Hamilton exerted his influence to ensure that the final constitutional settlement would incorporate some elements of the British system, in the interests of political and social stability. However, in his remarkable multiple careers as soldier, lawyer and politician, Hamilton never undertook a theoretical work whose breadth could compare to the *Reflections*, which perhaps explains why his ideological allegiance is still contested.

Despite these ambiguities, it is reasonable to summarize the conservative case against the French Revolution as one which was antipathetic to principles which would now be recognized as *liberal* in nature. Contrasting views of human nature lay at the heart of this dispute – liberals believed that human beings were susceptible to improvement (even to 'perfection'), in keeping with the Enlightenment emphasis on the potential advantages which could arise from the cultivation of 'reason'. For their part, conservatives doubted whether humanity could ever 'progress' in real terms, since most people would always be swayed by 'passion' directed to one object or another, and (in spite of Plato's hopes) even the best educated individual would be prone to egregious errors. The work of the British poet and philosopher Samuel Taylor Coleridge (1772–1834: see Chapter 7) is particularly instructive in this context.

Unlike Burke or Hamilton, Coleridge never aspired to a political career; but in his early days his enthusiasm for the ideas of the French Revolution inspired a dream of emigration to the United States, where he and his friends would establish a utopian community, in which (among other things) they would regard marriage as a token of affection which could be honoured or broken in accordance with changing moods. However, when Britain's security was threatened by the prospect of a French invasion via Ireland, Coleridge reassessed his position. Tacitly accepting Burke's charge that intellectuals had endangered their country by judging its practices against unrealizable standards, Coleridge argued that a loosely defined body of opinion-leaders – the 'clerisy' – should enhance political and social stability by illustrating the importance of shared cultural and institutional traditions. In other words, there is a good case for arguing that Coleridge underwent an ideological 'conversion' – from a broadly liberal outlook to a conservative viewpoint.

Coleridge (again unlike Burke in this respect) was highly sensitive to the possibility that technological change would prove a more potent threat to the conservative world view than the speculative writings of French ideologues. From this perspective, it could be argued that conservatism, as a practical basis for political action, was beginning to lose its persuasive power at around the time of its most eloquent and systematic articulation. Wherever it took root, the process of industrialization had obvious potential to undermine the rural, 'organic' society whose continuance had been a crucial presupposition for Burke, as for earlier 'conservatives' like Ibn Khaldun. It was not *inevitable* that the rapid transition to a mechanical, urban-based populace would result in the replacement of traditional structures of authority by democratic institutions. As Daniel Ziblatt has argued, within Europe, the establishment of democratic governance depended crucially on the attitude of the old elites. In Britain, conservatives (most, but not all of whom supported the upper-case 'Conservative' Party, which adopted the name in 1834) took the path of minimal resistance, and by the 1860s the party had accepted the extension of political participation to the level of organizing itself for a fight for mass support against the Liberals.[3] In France, and (especially) Germany, the acceptance of democracy was grudging at best. In every case, however, the process of acceptance marked a defeat for conservatism as a distinctive ideology. Formal equality in terms of civil rights, notably the ability to vote, could be accepted by conservatives on the understanding that the effects would be tempered (if not completely undermined) by the workings of an economic system in which the old elites retained their dominant position; but even this was eroded by the emerging liberal idea of 'meritocracy', against which hereditary privilege could find no persuasive arguments.

As a result, while the ideological identity of thinkers up to the mid-nineteenth century is open to dispute between commentators who take special interest in such matters, after that time the question of definition becomes fraught with unavoidable difficulties. In the United States, the problem seemed less onerous, since the stable, hierarchical order envisaged by Burke had never taken root – indeed, one could argue that the inhabitants of the thirteen colonies took up arms *against* the kind of sociopolitical settlement which Burke's writings extolled.

This suggests that 'conservatism', as a distinctive ideology, has always been alien to the American ethos, making it more noteworthy that conservative-minded politicians like Alexander Hamilton were able to negotiate a constitutional balance which could guard against 'the tyranny of the majority'. On the other hand, if conservatism is closely related to respect for cultural and political traditions, it seems possible to effect reconciliation between conservatism and liberalism in the unique US context. An American 'conservative', on this view, is someone who wants to preserve cultural and political traditions which have always been predominantly *liberal* in nature. The remaining problem is why contemporary Americans should wish to identify themselves as 'conservatives', rather than being content with the Republican party label. This phenomenon can be explained by the fact that 'conservatism' emerged as a prominent element of debate in the United States after 1945 – that is, in the context of the Cold War. After the descent of the 'Iron Curtain', a key consideration in US politics at the national level was whether or not one could be considered to be 'soft on Communism'. Hardliners (regardless of party) adopted the word 'conservative' to distinguish them from their soft-hearted 'liberal' contemporaries. The label appealed across party boundaries, and was also applied to southern Democrats who sought to defend their distinctive traditions.

By 1945, most of the self-styled 'conservatives' in Europe had reached a broadly similar position, albeit by a very different route. The war of 1914–18 had been a catastrophe for the 'Burkean' conservative position, in the supposedly 'victorious' states as well as on the losing side. The old hereditary elites had blundered into a 'total war' which discredited their political leadership, as well as denuding their ranks through the sacrifice of the next generation of aristocrats in profitless combat. Ironically, in Europe, the First World War had a marked tendency to foster a 'conservative' mindset, in that many individuals who had previously endorsed Enlightenment optimism had been forced to recognize the possibility that human 'progress' did not necessarily imply increased happiness. But since much of the adult population of Europe had been mobilized for war – and millions had died – it was now increasingly difficult to sustain the conservative argument against liberal democratic institutions. If conflict in the fields of Flanders meant the levelling of distinctions of rank (or indeed of merit) through the use of bullets, a more positive application of the same principle should extended it to ballots in the post-war order.

Thus, between 1918 and 1945, Europeans who rejected the premises of individualistic liberal rationalism were essentially faced with two choices. In the wake of the 1917 Bolshevik Revolution they could follow the US model, and argue in a style which tacitly accepted an overlap between liberalism and conservatism – that is, they could continue (as in the British case) to call themselves 'Conservative', even though in ideological terms they would have to operate within liberal institutions, and run for elected office on policy programmes which promised to provide 'the greatest happiness for the greatest number'. Alternatively, they could continue to hanker after an effectual antidote both to liberalism and communism. In some notorious cases (e.g. Martin Heidegger and Carl Schmitt), this brought them into close proximity (or worse) with movements like the German National Socialists. Once the Nazis had been defeated, conservatives in West Germany and other liberated countries could seek a safe haven in Christian Democracy (see Chapter 12). Parties which accepted this label offered the prospect of political and social stability after the tumultuous years since 1914, thanks to their anchorage in long-established religious communities and a consensual approach to industrial relations. The prominence of Christian Democrats in European politics coincided with a period of remarkable economic prosperity, and they were at the forefront of moves to end centuries of European conflict through economic and political union.

American leadership of the 'free world' after 1945 ensured a considerable degree of transatlantic terminological spillover, encouraging the tendency to dub vehement European anti-communists as 'conservatives', even if (as in the case of Christian Democrats) they had accepted liberal free-market principles. In France, at least, opponents of liberalism could rally around the war hero Charles de Gaulle, whose determination to lead a national revival was unconstrained by the usual ideological considerations, and who accepted support from all quarters (like the novelist André Malraux, who had previously regarded himself as a Marxist). De Gaulle's self-evident patriotism, and his embodiment of traditional French institutions (the state, the Catholic Church and the army) ensured that he could command considerable support from conservatives even as the country underwent the painful transition from a fading global power to a potent force within Europe (see Chapter 14).

In this respect, de Gaulle invites comparison with the other two 'practitioners' featured in this volume. It is possible to identify some similarities between the former soldier de Gaulle and the ex-actor Ronald Reagan (see Chapter 15), although it is unlikely that either of them would have felt flattered by the association. But, in their very different countries, both were capable of offering reassurance in an insecure environment. To his opponents on both sides of the Atlantic, Reagan was a doctrinaire economic liberal, who, while claiming to be patriotic, polarized his country along ideological lines. However, a 'conservative' reading of Reagan's career is possible if one takes account of the strongly liberal traditions of his country and his pragmatic recognition of the limits of political possibilities.

Margaret Thatcher, however, is a more contentious case (see Chapter 16). If conservative supporters of Ronald Reagan could argue that he was merely reaffirming at the national level ideas which had a long and uninterrupted history in numerous US states, Thatcher's critics could portray her as a relentless radical, a reactionary, or both. In the name of economic liberalism, she sought to 'roll back the state' from its previous interventionist economic role; but at the same time, she was prepared to use legislation in the hope of re-animating values which, on her own reckoning, had been undermined since the apogee of enterprise, prosperity and virtue in the Victorian era. This can be seen as an attempt to bring Britain into conformity with Reagan's vision for the United States – that is, to sweep away any obstacles to the free play of 'market forces' in the economic arena, while trying to reverse changes in moral thinking which had occurred over previous decades. The obvious problem for Thatcher was that in Britain (unlike the United States), this programme depended on the application of force against recalcitrant groups, particularly the trade unions. Thatcher's belief that such methods were compatible with a resolute defence of liberty in other respects is aptly summarized in the title of Andrew Gamble's classic account – *The Free Economy and the Strong State*.[4] From the perspective of the present volume, a more damaging criticism of Thatcher was delivered by her erstwhile supporter John Gray, who argued that no political party which embraced free-market liberalism could possibly be regarded as 'conservative', since its economic approach was a recipe for incessant instability; indeed, in the context of 'globalization', the application of such ideas would undermine the cultural and legal prerequisites of liberalism itself.[5] However, Thatcher, like Reagan, can be portrayed as a politician who, in her first term of office at least, was more concerned with pragmatic 'problem-solving' than with a 'war of ideas'.[6]

The notion that Reagan and Thatcher were ideological liberals who, consciously or not, identified with 'conservatism' only because the word conveyed connotations of stability which were electorally useful, seems to apply in reverse to post-war Japan, which has been governed for most of the period since 1945 by a party whose name translates as 'Liberal Democrat', but which is usually designated (especially in media reports) as 'conservative'. In this instance, the ideological terminology looks even less helpful than usual, since the LDP has been a favoured vehicle for US influence over Japan, which enjoyed something akin to the West German 'economic miracle' thanks to the party's liberal policies. 'Japanese conservatism', on this showing, implies an acceptance of the constitution imposed by the United States in 1947. Yet it would be at least equally plausible to identify 'conservatism in Japan' with *resistance* to that constitution, whose provisions entailed a radical change from pre-war practices and institutional arrangements (see Chapter 11).

Turkey also experienced a radical change after the defeat of the Ottoman Empire in the First World War. In some respects, Kemal Ataturk could be compared to General de Gaulle – a nationalist who would adopt any policy which promised to promote national revival. However, unlike de Gaulle, Ataturk showed contempt, rather than empathy, for his nation's traditions; his desire to repress Islam, rather than trying to co-opt it into his enterprise, suggests an outlook which is impossible to square with any tenable definition of 'conservatism' (see Chapter 13). The secular regime maintained by Ataturk's successors was resisted by a variety of forces, none of which could find a formula which would allow them to make headway under the terms of the constitution. This situation was transformed after 2001, with the formation of the Justice and Development Parti (AKP). This movement, drawing support from several existing Islamic parties, presented itself to the Turkish electorate and the world as a 'conservative-democratic' party. On closer inspection, its stated ideals were reminiscent of Christian Democratic parties within the European Union which Turkey, at the time, was anxious to join. As such, in ideological terms, it projected a mixture of conservatism (respect for tradition) and liberalism (acceptance of the free market, tempered by welfare provisions). At the time of writing (November 2017), one might conclude that the party's principles were either inapplicable to the Turkish context or that they were proclaimed as part of a tactical ruse to disguise the real intention of restoring an Islamic state inspired by nostalgic memories of the Ottoman Empire.

Thus, three of the four geographical case studies included in this volume could be seen as complementary: European Christian Democracy, 'conservatism in Japan', and the AKP's 'conservative-democracy' in Turkey reflect, in varying degrees, the consequences of defeat in the wars of the twentieth century. The exceptional case, among our case studies, is Russia (Chapter 10). While the political and cultural heritage of the United States is heavily interlaced with liberalism, Russia's encounter with that ideology has been fleeting at best. Whatever its effect on Russian citizens, this experience has at least fostered a relatively continuous tradition of writing which could be described as authentically conservative – even if distinguished authors (like Aleksandr Solzhenitzyn) were forced to express their views in exile during the Soviet era. This tradition is marked by a strong streak of fatalism, which might encourage an acceptance of President Putin's regime as distinctively 'conservative', in the Russian context. Others, no doubt, will regard it as a blend of market liberalism and authoritarianism, and thus just one of many contemporary examples of a state which exhibits nothing more than a superficial semblance of stability.

The principle of selection for this volume – both in terms of subjects and contributors – could have been dictated by a desire to promote one particular understanding of conservatism. That approach, however, would have created a highly misleading impression of the academic discipline, as well as running the risk of distorting the subject matter. The alternative is to accept the disagreements over definitions and attributions, and to compile a volume which allows readers to make up their own minds.[7] The subjects have been chosen from examples which are commonly supposed to display 'conservative' characteristics, and the contributors are recognized authorities, who were given a licence to develop their own arguments rather than being asked to adhere to any specific interpretation of conservatism. There has not even been an attempt to impose uniformity in the use of upper- or lower-case 'c' in relation to 'conservatism', since disagreement on this matter is merely a symptom of the ongoing dispute over definitions and thus an unfortunate occupational hazard.

The chapters can be read as free-standing contributions to the existing literature on the various thinkers and themes. Hopefully, though, most readers will tackle the book as a whole, and end up thinking that although a sieve seems a less promising receptacle than a leaky bucket, it can have its uses: like gold prospectors of the old school, they could find themselves in possession of some valuable nuggets.

PART ONE

Early moments

CHAPTER ONE

Authority and conservatism in Plato's *Republic*

Joseph M. Ellis and Casey R. Pratt

The *Republic*

Book VIII

Liberty makes its way into private households and in the end it breeds anarchy even among the animals. – What do you mean?

I mean, for example, that a father will accustom himself to behave like a child and to fear his sons, while the son behaves like a father, and feels neither shame nor fear before his parents, in order to be free. A resident alien is the equal of a citizen and a citizen the equal of a resident alien, and so too a foreign visitor. – This is what happens.

Yes it does, I said, and so do other such small matters. A teacher in such a community is afraid of his pupils and flatters them, while the pupils think little of their teachers or their tutors. Altogether the young are thought to be the equals of the old and compete with them in word and deed, while the old accommodate themselves to the young, and are full of playfulness and pleasantries, thus aping the young for fear of appearing disagreeable and authoritarian.[1]

Plato's *Republic* is the first thoroughgoing exploration of political philosophy on record. His work captures the conversations of his great teacher, Socrates (c. 470–399 BC) on the question of justice: what it is, and how a society can be constructed to provide for it. The *Republic* is divided into ten 'books' – or chapters – and in each book, Socrates and his various interlocutors work through this question of justice. Book VIII, in particular, is a fascinating chapter for political scientists, as it lays out a theory of regime evolution which appears relevant to today's political environment. It is also a fascinating chapter for conservatives, chiefly on the question of authority. While we should be cautious in assigning to Socrates the identity of a conservative icon, an analysis of Plato's written work and Socrates' spoken words has much to contribute to conservative discourse. Some of these ideas are apparent in the writings of Edmund Burke and Michael Oakeshott, for example (see Chapters 5 and 9).

We devote the first section of this essay to analysing Socrates' thinking on the question of authority, democracy and tyranny. In this section, attention is paid to Socrates' understanding of fathers and teachers in relation to authority, and the dangers which can arise from rejecting such authority figures. In the second section, we examine Book VIII in relation to conservatism, and how Socrates' ideas on authority might speak to our historical understanding of conservatism. In the final section, we conclude with some germane thoughts regarding the current state of conservatism and its relation to authority, in particular within the context of modern American conservatism.

In Book VII, Socrates defines the ideal regime type: a polity ruled by an aristocracy of philosopher kings. Socrates says that 'they will attach the greatest importance to doing what is right and to the honors deriving from that; they will regard justice as the greatest and most essential thing' (540e). The entire trajectory of the *Republic* builds to this moment, when Socrates lays out once and for all what the just regime looks like. By Book VIII, however, Socrates had turned his attention to the degeneration of this ideal. The above quotation (562e–563b) examines the devolution from democracy to tyranny, where ultimate freedom is traded for ultimate authority. Socrates' description of democracy is laudatory in part, but highly critical overall. He regards democracy as a regime which promotes both liberty and, in its own way, mob rule; indeed, it was this very mob that would imprison him, and eventually put him to death. But Socrates also notes that democracy is the only regime type where philosophers are genuinely free to live their lives. On this diversity and variety, Socrates remarks: 'This is the most beautiful of all constitutions. Like a cloak embroidered with every kind of ornament, so this city, embroidered with every kind of character, would seem the most beautiful, and perhaps many would judge it to be so, like children and women gazing at embroideries of many colors' (557c–557d). But the variety gives way to permissiveness, because individuals will not feel compelled to abide by any single source of authority, or 'be ruled if [they] do not want to be' (557e). This permissiveness will lead to its downfall: order will collapse, and in that search for order, the mob will reach out to a strong 'protector' to repair what ails them.

Socrates' use of a father figure and a school teacher to catalogue this collapse of order is an important moment in the book. Traditionally, the father or teacher would be significant sources of authority. Socrates asks, hypothetically, 'What do you think will happen in a society where no one obeys their father or teacher?' This is a timeless and universal question, in the sense that societies have always depended on parents and educators of one sort or another to shape future generations. Perhaps it could be argued that fathers specifically, or teachers generally, are not always the best at doing this. But no one would dispute the historical significance of either role. For instance, in fifth century BC, *The Analects of Confucius* recorded a student asking, 'whether there were any form of encouragement by which he could induce the common people to be respectful and loyal'?[2]

What invests fathers and teachers with authority? The implication from Socrates is that they possess a degree of maturity, experience and, ultimately, wisdom. In degenerating to tyranny, Socrates notes that a father will behave like a child in trying to appease his child, and the child will in turn dominate the father and rebuke his power. Likewise, the teacher will come to fear his students, and instruct in such a way that the student is placated rather than educated. Grube's translation uses the word 'aping' to describe this process, whereby the elders will imitate the 'playfulness' of the younger generation in attempting to connect with them and appear less 'authoritarian.' However, the more the father or teacher descends to the level of the child, the less the child will accept him or her.

Leo Strauss (see Chapter 8) suggests that while the specifics of the political situation in Athens are unknown to the reader of the *Republic*, the conversations take place in an 'era of political decay'.[3] This decay did not happen all at once, hence the need to describe the degeneration of the political process. Like the regimes Socrates documented, the collapse of the institutions of parenting and teaching is the result of a slow but theoretically inevitable deterioration. These institutions are developed over time, by a gradual process which creates two distinct populations: father/child, or teacher/student. Democracy, as Socrates understands it, begins to level that relationship, and in doing so, casts out a traditionally important source of authority.

Why fathers and teachers *should* have authority is a complex question. It would be too simple to say that fathers or educators are *naturally* more authoritative according to Socrates, and thus deserve the respect of the child strictly by the nature of the relationship. In the beginning of the *Republic*, his first conversation is with Cephalus, an old man. Socrates tells Cephalus that he 'enjoys conversing with men of advanced years', and wants to learn from the path taken by those who came before him, such as a father, implying that knowledge can be gained by experiences (328e). Moreover,

Socrates recognizes that fathers in particular can be important teachers and role models for children.

In both *Apology* and *Crito*, Socrates is acutely aware of the lesson he would teach his own sons by his actions in the court of law, and later, in prison. He admits in those dialogues, in so many words, that engaging in an injustice would undermine his authority as a father. In *Crito*, he describes how his own parents raised him to obey the laws of the city, and how he raised his own sons to obey those same laws.[4] He also encourages the crowd to hold his sons to a high standard, saying in the *Apology*: 'When my sons grow up, avenge yourselves by causing them the same kind of grief that I caused you, if you think they care for money or anything else more than they care for virtue, or if they think they are somebody when they are nobody.'[5]

Without fathers and teachers, where will the son or student turn for authority and leadership? Socrates' view is that the search for authority will lead to a tyrant, though every member of the community will set off on different paths in the last vestiges of democracy. It begins with a society that divides itself into three parts: the idlers, the money makers, and the people. The idlers do nothing and appreciate the liberty of the democratic society, the money makers obsess over wealth and the people, who work with their hands, are at first non-political, and have few possessions. As the money makers seek to control society, however, the people will resist, and they will elevate one man above the others to protect them from this threat.

Initially, Socrates renders a sympathetic portrait of such a man. Socrates refers to him as the 'people's champion,' someone who protects the middle classes from the wealthy. But, the more the tyrant is elevated, the more his thirst for power becomes insatiable. Socrates says: '[T]he man who has tasted human flesh, a single piece of it cut up among the pieces from other sacrificial victims, must inevitably become a wolf' (565d–565e). As this one man protects them, he will highlight the 'enemies' of the people, prosecute and order power around himself, all the while distributing resources to the people who put him in power. A snapshot of such a character – named Thrasymachus – is revealed in Book I of the *Republic*.

Thrasymachus is the representation of brute power in the *Republic*. His version of justice is something to the effect of *might makes right*. Thrasymachus argues that justice lies in obeying the rulers, and making your opponents weak. Such a notion of justice results in the ruler's continued authority over the subjects (339d, 340b). But Socrates turns the tables on Thrasymachus when he notes that the best leaders rule on behalf of their subjects. The shepherd is successful because he uses his authority to care for his sheep, not simply to use the authority to abuse them. This causes Thrasymachus to blush, and ultimately to agree with Socrates that a 'just man ... [is] wise and good, and the unjust resembles the bad and ignorant' (350c).

The notion that justice is related not only to goodness, but also wisdom, brings us back to the significance of the father. In an earlier portion of

Book VIII, Socrates describes the dilemmas facing a young son in a society which exalts meddlers and boasters, but ignores those who mind their own business. What should the young boy do? Socrates instructs that while 'the young man sees and hears all this … he also listens to what his father says, observes what he does from close at hand, and compares his actions with those of others'. Moreover, while the young man is pulled multiple ways by society, the father 'nourishes the reasonable part of the soul' (550b). The father becomes a central figure in Socrates' dialogue on the question of wisdom, how it is preserved and how it is passed down. These are the very same questions that conservatives like Edmund Burke and Michael Oakeshott would ask some 2,000 years later.

It can be unwise to make modern political assessments of historic texts and thinkers. There is a danger of making Socrates (or any classic thinker) out to be a spokesperson for one's pet political project, whether that be conservatism, liberalism, communism, fascism, and the like. In reading the *Republic*, a book in which marriage is abolished, property is shared and there is a rigorous division of the social classes, it would be hard to describe Socrates as a type of conservative in any modern sense of that word. Yet, there are aspects of the book which speak to modern political problems, especially problems identified by conservatives.

In Book VIII, Socrates laments the loss that occurs when fathers and teachers – trying to conserve and pass down tradition and knowledge from past generations – find their authority questioned and their speeches ignored. This idea of a slow but gradual process, whereby maturity, experience and wisdom are created, is the starting point for most conservative perspectives in understanding what makes society work. This view of conservatism comes from the writings of Edmund Burke, when he was lamenting the downfall of tradition and stability in France amid the upheaval of the French Revolution. Burke's *Reflections on the Revolution in France* depicts a political environment in which the traditional sources of authority, such as the family, the church and the school, are eradicated in favor of abstract principles, such as liberty. In doing so, society is left with 'no compass to govern [itself], nor can we know distinctly to what port [to] steer'.[6] The analogy of an aimless ship is illustrative, insofar as wisdom passed down over generations is a crucial means for navigating human existence. These traditions also promote restraint and a degree of caution.

Yuval Levin, in *The Great Debate*, highlights the Burkean idea that 'prudence is a function of experience and education'.[7] Prudence, coupled with judgment, keeps individuals safe from the excesses of an overly atomized society disconnected from traditional institutions. Levin notes that:

> Breaking apart all the connections that stand between the individual and the state and leaving equal but separate individuals alone would expose them to the raw power of the state directly. The people would also have no protection from one another or from the mass of citizens, in such a

situation. Burke worries that this would leave them unable to defend their freedoms and subject to even more brutal and dangerous abuses of power than the ancient despotisms could be capable of. The social institutions that stand between the individual and the government are crucial barriers to the ruthlessness of public officials and the occasional cruelty of majorities. They are essential to liberty.[8]

Levin's remarks correspond to Socrates' fears. Fathers and teachers provide a type of bulwark against the power of the state. Once those 'social institutions' are removed, reliance on domineering political actors is more likely. The tyrant becomes a stand-in for other potential authority figures.

However, tyranny does not have to proceed just with bad actors, either. Good people come along who speak with perfectly reasonable intentions that can, in turn, however, reject traditional, more conservative ideas. Burkean Conservatism's most articulate spokesperson in the twentieth century was British educator Michael Oakeshott. In his essay 'Rationalism in Politics,' Oakeshott recognizes one of the more pernicious problems in contemporary European society as the ever-present 'Rationalist'. The Rationalist, according to Oakeshott, values reason above all other principles, shirking tradition, habit and prejudice. Oakeshott wrote:

> His mental attitude is at once skeptical and optimistic: skeptical, because there is no opinion, no habit, no belief, nothing so firmly rooted or so widely held that he hesitates to question it and to judge it by what he calls 'reason'; optimistic, because the Rationalist never doubts the power of his 'reason' … to determine the truth of an opinion or the propriety of an action.[9]

The simultaneously sceptical *and* optimistic person is a perfect description of the youth in the latter stages of Socrates' construction of democracy. Sceptical is an appropriate word in the sense that no father or teacher could possibly have knowledge worthy to be attained by the son or pupil. The outlook is optimistic in the belief that the young can do it on their own, not needing the advice or wisdom of others. Reading Oakeshott and Plato together, we should by no means conclude that reason is bad, or should be rejected outright. Reason is a prerequisite for learning philosophy, after all. But the Rationalist use of reason can become something of a battering ram to dominate others. A person driven by reason might have a type of authority, for example, but he or she might also be deficient in something like wisdom or experience. Thus, even a cursory glance at the young son in Book VIII would be a troubling turn of events for conservatives in the tradition of Burke, or Oakeshott, among others.

Moreover, as Strauss pointed out, the regime types Socrates defines are not so much ideologies as they are a composition of a political community. As Strauss wrote: '[Socrates] is concerned with the character of each kind of regime and with the end which it manifestly and explicitly pursues.' Strauss goes on to write that democracy's downfall is that the end it pursues is 'not virtue but freedom, i.e., the freedom to live either nobly or basely according to one's liking'.[10] One could, for example, make the argument that the son has much to teach the father, and certainly anyone who has ever taught a class understands how much our own students can teach us. That would seem noble. But Socrates does not see democracy approaching a noble outcome. The youth will be driven to excesses, and those excesses will mark the collapse of the democratic order.

It is important to restate that Socrates' position as some type of conservative figurehead greatly overstates his place among conservative thinkers. As an ideological movement, conservatism was not expressed in any meaningful way until the eighteenth and nineteenth centuries, and even then, had a tenuous relationship with ancient philosophy. Modern conservatism would especially reject the 'communal' arrangements recommended in the *Republic*. That said, in two very important respects, Socrates – by way of Plato's writing – has much to offer conservatism. First, the idea of authority coupled with the institutions of family and schooling is central to Socrates' thinking in Book VIII, and representative of concerns conservatives have long had about the rejection of traditional forms of authority. Second, Socrates was gravely concerned about political arrangements, which at first appear to be in the best interest of the people, to only subvert that interest over time. This is how he and many Greeks would have understood democracy during their era.

For example, the recent presidential election in the United States represented the variety, diversity and perhaps the beauty inherent in democracy. The election of Donald Trump pulled from the sidelines those whom the political establishment had abandoned. It was an election that gave many hope after years of being ignored. But his election also deeply concerned many Americans who were worried that it reflected a troubling slide into a more authoritarian, or tyrannical, moment. For these critics, he is a tyrant-in-waiting, taking advantage of the democratic structures of society to coalesce his power.

This criticism is overwrought. The United States has persevered, despite civil war, political scandal and serious ideological divisions, and will maintain democratic features long after Trump leaves office. Yet, Trump is an interesting political figure, not least because although he is perhaps not a traditional conservative in the heritage of Burke or Oakeshott, he has successfully maneuvered conservatism – at least in America – to something to fit his world view. This world view is based on a certain idea of authority that does not square with Socrates, and has little use for fathers or teachers. Trump's worldview is much closer to that of Thrasymachus, that to be authoritative is to be tough, stubborn and in charge, but not necessarily wise or particularly experienced. Again, this does not mean that Trump or Thrasymachus are textbook tyrants. And Trump is neither the first American president nor will he be the last to tangle with the media, the judiciary and members of Congress. But through Socrates' dialogue with Thrasymachus, and his remarks in Book VIII, a composite sketch of a very perilous political character begins to take shape. Trump may not be the tyrant, but at minimum, he has come along at a time when all of the traditional sources of authority – parents, teachers, elected officials, journalists, even religious leaders – are seen as woefully inept guideposts for society.

Socrates' description of the transition from democratic government to tyranny is undoubtedly both provocative and instructive, especially for students of modern political philosophy. The people selected their protector for his strength, and while his strength was deployed in strict alignment with the interests of the people, perhaps the people were satisfied that democracy had once again righted itself. But, through a process compared to 'the legend that is told of the shrine of Lycaean Zeus in Arcadia' (565d–566a), the strong protector transforms into a tyrant; the same strength that effectively protected the people from the plundering of the wealthy class now becomes a terrible source of persecution. If Socrates does not articulate quite clearly enough to satisfy us precisely on when and how the transformation takes place, he has at least pointed us toward the key questions: from whom do we seek authority, and why; and, following an attempt to reform that problem, how much authority – how much strength – is helpful and just? And how much is dangerous?

CHAPTER TWO

St Augustine's 'two cities' – antidote for modern secular progressivism?

W. J. Coats

Thus the things necessary for this mortal life are used by both kinds of men and families alike, but each has its own ... widely different aim in using them. The earthly city, which does not live by faith, seeks an earthly peace, and the end it proposes, in the well-ordered concord of civic obedience and rule, is the combination of men's wills to attain the things which are helpful to this life. The heavenly city, or rather the part of it which sojourns on earth and lives by faith, makes use of this peace only because it must, until this mortal condition ... shall pass away. Consequently ... it lives like a captive and stranger in the earthly city .... Even the heavenly city ... while in its state of pilgrimage, avails itself of the peace of earth ... and makes this earthly peace bear upon the peace of heaven ...[1]

Whoever hopes ... great good in this world, and in this earth, his wisdom is folly. Can anyone think it was fulfilled in the peace of Solomon's reign .... For none other reigned in such great peace as he; nor did that nation ever hold that kingdom so as to have

no anxiety lest it should be subdued by enemies; for in the very
great mutability of human affairs such great security is never
given to any people, that it should not dread invasions hostile to
this life. Therefore the place of this promised peaceful and secure
habitation is eternal . . .[2]
If there is some choice ... here, such as we understand from the
words 'a remnant that was chosen by grace', the choice is not of
those who, for the sake of eternal life, have been made righteous.
It is, rather, that those are chosen who are to be made righteous,
and this choice is so very hidden that it can by no means be
discerned by us who are in the same lump . . . . And yet what
shall we say? Is there injustice with God? Of course not! *Yet why*
is one person treated one way and another person another way
. . . . Inscrutable are his judgments and unfathomable his ways.
(Romans, 11:33)[3]

If the North African Catholic bishop, Augustine of Hippo (354–430), could be considered a 'conservative' in modern terminology (there were no ideological parties in Roman politics), the basis for the association would lie in his pessimistic view of human nature and human understanding, and his belief that the future would grow increasingly corrupt. On the theory that modern political concepts are secularized theological ones, the contemporary student of politics will hopefully gain insight into the origins of the 'conservative vs. progressive' divide by following the way in which Augustine's idea of two distinct kinds of human beings and human destinies were conflated over centuries into a single category by those unable to accept Augustine's pessimism: those impelled by their hopes to believe that 'the arc of history' tends towards earthly justice. How did this occur?

As he aged (and as the Roman empire continued to disintegrate), Augustine moved in his search for truth from a kind of Platonism (in which 'progress' was an individual ascent to pure intellect) to a mystical Christianity as the context for all human striving, grounded in faith in unique historical events – the incarnation and crucifixion of Jesus. These events broke the cyclical pagan view of the passage of time for Augustine, and substituted a *spiritual* eschatology tending towards a final redemptive event for those providentially and mysteriously elected or chosen by God. This viewpoint was partnered by a change in which Augustine declined to view biblical prophecy exclusively in a literal sense (as had the ancient Hebrews in their search for an earthly messiah), and moved towards a more allegorical or figurative interpretation of prophecy, whether of the Old or New Testament, whether of 'Daniel' or of 'Revelation'.

All of this flowed from Augustine's conviction that there were two types of human souls – those presented by God's grace with the choice to participate in a heavenly redemption and peace by placing God first in their lives, and those (inscrutably for us) not so chosen, who were to remain eternally in a condition of strife and pain. One novelty of Augustine's mature view on these two 'cities' or societies made up of these two types of souls was that they were not participating in the same 'eschatology', though they were mixed together in the realm of change (the *saeculum*) until a final redemptive event, and were each using it for their own respective purposes.

The contrast between Augustine's views here and modern secular progressivism hinged on a new interpretation of Augustine's belief that human beings, seeing 'through a glass darkly,' were not intellectually capable of discerning clearly God's providential plan for secular history, and that there would be no intermediate millennium or gradual elimination of evil on the planet. This interpretation was furnished by makers of English-speaking reformed Christianity – John Milton, Joseph Mede, Jonathan Edwards, and others – who returned to the Hebraic and arguably biblical view that God's designs and approbations could be read in history and seconded and partnered by collective human action. While this development was arguably prefigured when Aquinas brought Aristotle into the Church and treated the state and coercive power as natural (rather than 'fallen'), it was the English-speaking Protestant divines (especially in America) who conflated Augustine's dualistic eschatology of the two 'cities' into a single eschatology, in which they could read in secular history God's approval of their project incrementally to transform the earthly city into the heavenly city, through social and political reforms worldwide.

Although initially a Protestant Christian development, this millennialist[4] project for the progressive, aggregate-increasing amelioration of evil on the planet ultimately became an anti-Christian movement in the writings of Comte, Marx and others, treating 'Providence' as simply a universal human reason. But that is a different story. In this brief survey, I simply attempt to offer an interpretation of what Augustine means by his dualistic eschatology, and what have been the problematic effects of conflating it into a single, immanentist secular eschatology. Let us turn now to the inspection of our selected texts.

Our first text is from Chapter 17 of Book XIX of Augustine's magnum opus, *The City of God*, a rhetorical work years in the making, intended to refute the contemporary view that the Roman Empire was collapsing because its adoption of Christianity had made it 'soft' and disorganized. The work also provides implicitly a view of world history as interpreted through biblical and prophetic lenses. In the selected passage, Augustine is describing the relations between two distinct kinds of human beings and their associations or societies. The 'earthly city' refers to non-believers who seek to use the things of the world for utility and enjoyment as ends in themselves. The 'heavenly city' refers to those who live 'by faith' and use the things of the world, insofar as necessary, as pilgrims passing through it, until their mortal condition shall pass away. (The 'heavenly city' also refers to those souls which have already given up the mortal coil.) For both kinds of persons, earthly peace and order are desirable, though for different reasons. For members of the 'earthly city', peace is desirable for the enjoyment of earthly things as a goal or aim. For Augustine, this attempt constitutes a perversion or dis-ordering – one should *use* things of *utility*, and one should enjoy the objects of enjoyment, not attempt merely to use them. Said differently, enjoyment is properly delight in things which are by their nature ends in themselves. The members of the 'heavenly city' attempt to do just that while on their earthly pilgrimage to strengthen their faith.

Yet, these two types of individuals and societies both desire peace and civic order, and this common need provides a basis or overlap for living together, as well as a conception of the political state. Members of the 'heavenly city' are to be thankful for the peace provided by the state for their earthly pilgrimage, and accord it just as much obligation as is warranted, including even military service in a just war. There is, however, no implication here of the view that political life has any positive role in the growth of the personality as in the Aristotelian and Ciceronian accounts, or as in the attempted Aquinian synthesis of nature and grace. Government and private property remain both a punishment and partial remedy for 'fallen' human nature. For Augustine, as for St Paul,[5] the spiritual person is not the *psychikos*, who seeks contentment of the *psyche* or animal soul, and participates in political life as part of that quest.

Also important to note here for our purposes is that Augustine declines to identify the 'heavenly city' with any earthly association such as the Church (and certainly not the Roman Empire). The Church has an important role to play in the social lives of believers and in keeping alive the Christian message: but it is not the 'heavenly city,' a mystical union of believers which cannot be certainly identified on earth. Members of the Church sometimes join for social status or 'temporal advantage.' And in the final days, Augustine speculates that corruption may be so rife that there may be more genuine believers on the outside of the Church than within it. To quote Hobbes in an Augustinian mood, 'for God only knoweth the heart'.[6]

In our second selected text, also from *The City of God* (BK XVII, 13), Augustine is cautioning against the 'folly' of hoping 'for any great good in this world' owing to 'the very great mutability of human affairs'. This includes even the hope for permanent peace and cessation of war, with Augustine noting that even in the relatively peaceful reign of King Solomon, there was still anxiety about external invasion. For Augustine, war on earth will never end, because it is rooted in the earthly battle between the flesh and the spirit, and this will not change until the end of time. For Augustine, there will never come a time when the lion shall lie down with the lamb, and men beat their swords into ploughshares.

Hence, believers are called upon to serve in just wars to preserve the community of believers (and not for the potentially selfish aim of individual preservation).[7] The issue here is the spirit or frame of mind in which the believers take up arms. If not done in a spirit of hate, lust or vainglory, it is at least preferable to see the community of believers destroyed. Augustine even justified the use of coercion towards perfectionist heretics such as Bishop Donatus on the grounds that it was for Donatus's own good, in restraining the bad effects of his influence on others.

In general, one can see Augustine's belief in the permanence of war as emblematic of the permanent tension between love of God and love of self (*superbia*) even in the souls of believers. Yet the 'falleness' of the world need not lead to 'moral paralysis' since on an individual basis there is always room for improvement in oneself and in one's relations with others. But faith in the cumulative amelioration of the human condition through institutions is not warranted, given the inherent perversity of the human will.

For Augustine, the ultimate source of evil is always in the 'will,' not in environmental or bodily influences. And though he sees humanity as 'fallen' (even newborn babies exhibit selfishness), the material world itself is not fallen, and there is nothing inherently corrupting in matter, as there was for Greek ontological dualists such as Plato. This is evident in the symbolism of the 'Incarnation' (the *logos* become flesh) as an advancement for humanity. The *saeculum* (the earthly realm of change) for Augustine can still remain as an arena for individual spiritual growth, so long as the human will can remain focused on God rather than self, but this is not to be hoped for through the progressive amelioration of public institutions, including even the Church.

In our third selected text, Augustine is writing to Bishop Simplician of Milan in response to queries on various subjects. In this particular instance, he reminds Simplician of the obscurity of God's way for us in the *saeculam*, citing St Paul in Romans, 11:33: 'inscrutable are his judgments and unfathomable his ways.' Augustine's point is that it is impossible for us, as 'fallen' beings, to understand why some are chosen to be made righteous and others not, but this does *not* mean there is 'injustice with God'. It is simply not given to us to fathom such things, for now 'we see through a glass darkly'.

His appreciation of the difficulty in discerning divine purposes in secular history[8] is also apparent in Augustine's increasingly allegorical interpretation of biblical prophecy in books such as *Daniel* and *Revelation*. For example, the binding of Satan for a millennium may simply mean a period when forces for good are dominant over forces for evil, and references to 'the beast' may simply mean the 'earthly city'. The point for our purpose is to recognize Augustine's appreciation of the dangers in thinking that we can ever know *with certainty* God's purposes in history, and who is chosen and who is not, who is on a pilgrimage to heaven and who is here to enjoy the earth for its own sake. As we shall see momentarily, the hallmark (and danger) of modern progressivist thought is the claim to know with certainty at least the broad outlines of where 'history' is going. Arguably, the modern totalitarian impulse arises in the conflation (and secularization) of two ideas which Augustine strains (not always successfully) to keep apart – the thoughts that 'I must be about God's work,' and, secondly, 'what *I* am doing is God's work, not what *you* are doing.'

Let us now turn briefly to how Augustine's teaching on the 'two cities' was modified to include the idea that 'the earthly city' could incrementally be transformed with human assistance into 'the heavenly city'; how the two separate destinies were conflated into one. There were always those who resisted Augustine's mystical reading of the respective destinies of the two 'cities' or peoples, and remained with the view of the Old Testament that the chosen people of God could be clearly identified and would prosper materially on earth when they followed God's commandments. Augustine's view that the 'earthly city' would always be supreme on earth was simply too dark to serve as the general orientation of medieval Christianity, especially after the thirteenth-century Aquinian synthesis of Athens and Jerusalem, and its positive view of political life as nourishing the moral virtues. In the *Universal History* (c. 1670) of the seventeenth-century French bishop and royal tutor, Jacques Bossuet, for example, we see no doubt that the people of God in history were the ancient Israelites,[9] and that the Roman Church was the inheritor of their covenant; nor is there any doubt about how to read God's providential plan as unfolding *in world history*:

> My principal intention was to make you consider … the progress of the people of God, and that of the great empires. *These two objects run together … and have, so to speak, one and the same course.*[10]

For Bossuet, all of this is simply asserted as obvious by inspection. But in seventeenth-century English Protestantism, we begin to see a careful re-examination of how to read the prophetic book of the New Testament, The Revelation of St. John, in the light of Hebraic readings of God in history. In brief, in the works of the Cambridge biblical scholar, Joseph Mede, and others, we begin to see a modification of Augustine's mystical, allegorical, and 'amillennialist' interpretation of prophecy to accommodate the view that one is not to use the peace provided by the state merely to ready one's soul for a final reunion with God, but also for the progressive elimination of evil worldwide, and with it the increasing practical success and material prosperity of the faithful. The idea even arose that believers could not only discern God's purposes but help God in their actualization in secular history – in a fashion similar, two centuries later, to Hegel's making explicit in the *Phenomenology* why *Geist* entered human history in the first place.[11]

Now there were several un-Augustinian features in these developments. First was the belief that 'fallen' human beings could discern with certitude divine purpose in human history; second, the belief that God would reward in discernible acts the faithful who followed divine law; third, the belief that the faithful or people of God could be clearly identified by their practical success. And finally, there was a literal interpretation of prophetic scripture to support the idea that Satan would be bound for a millennium, permitting the dominance of the 'heavenly city' over the 'earthly city,' and the progressive, incremental elimination of evil and an incremental spread of peace, harmony and material prosperity.

These un-Augustanian 'millennialist' beliefs found their way into English-speaking Protestantism both theologically and politically in the Liberal-Whig English tradition (following the failure of Cromwell), and into American Puritanism and the 'apocalyptic Whiggism' of President John Adams and, in time, the Progressive Movement under Professor and President Woodrow Wilson, who mis-read (through the lens of the American Social Gospel movement) John Calvin's political realism and strict separation of Augustine's 'two cities'.[12] Yet that Wilsonian Progressivism, though now secularized, still informs the domestic and foreign policy of the American democratic-progressivist outlook and its vision of the increasing, incremental amelioration of evil on the planet, even in some quarters to the point of displacing persuasive politics and political rhetoric with a pious 'ruling for Truth'[13] – an alternative which the West once characterized as a recipe for endless religious and ideological warfare following the cessation of the Thirty Years' War, and the establishment of the Westphalian international system in 1648. Arguably, Augustine identified a way to limit the potential tyranny in a moral posture flowing from *certainty* about the direction of linear history, once the Christian revelation had broken the cyclical pagan view of the passage of time. And it derived from Augustine's following the implications of the seven words, 'my Kingdom is not of this world.'

CHAPTER THREE

Conservatism and Ibn Khaldun

Allen J. Fromherz

*Group feeling ('asabiyya') produces the ability to defend oneself,
to offer opposition, to protect oneself, and to press one's claims.
Whoever loses it is too weak to do any of these things. The
subject of imposts and taxes belongs to this discussion of the
things that force meekness upon a tribe ... Imposts and taxes
are a sign of oppression and meekness that proud souls do not
tolerate, unless they consider (paying them) easier than being
killed and destroyed . . .*[1]
*It should be known that a quality belonging to perfection, which
tribes possessing group feeling are eager to cultivate and which
attests to their (right to) royal authority, is respect for scholars,
pious men, noble (relatives of the prophet), well-born persons,
and the different kinds of merchants and foreigners, as well as the
ability to assign everybody to his proper station.*[2]
*Luxury wears out royal authority and overthrows it. When a
dynasty is wiped out, power is taken from that dynasty by
those whose group feeling has a share in the (established or
pre-existing) group feeling, since it is recognized that people
submit and are subservient to (the established group feeling) ...
Eventually, a great change takes place in the world, such as the*

transformation of a religion, or the disappearance of a civilization, or something else willed by the power of God. Then, royal authority is (definitively) transferred from one group to another – to the one that God permits to effect that change.[3]

Ibn Khaldun (1333–1406) advised against planting orange trees. Orange trees, especially the Sevillian orange, known for its powerful and luxurious scent, risked moral and social decline. They did not bear edible fruit (anybody who has visited Seville to this day knows how bitter the oranges are). They are an ultimate symbol of what happens when the pleasures of urban life take over and weaken the 'natural' and divinely ordained state of humans. While part of a divine plan, civilization, like the Sevillian orange, contains the bitter seeds of its own destruction. Luxury enervates the body and the soul, making a dynasty and a people prey to more powerful, more cohesive groups, tribes on the outskirts of urban power. These tribes may know less, they may have primitive beliefs and understandings about the world, but they will prevail again and again over the urbane and the elite of the city. Yet there was more to Ibn Khaldun than the condemnation of orange trees and taxes (see the quotes above). We need to look deeply into his writing and his historical context to understand what his 'conservatism' may have meant.

Before discussing the 'conservatism' of Ibn Khaldun, the famed Tunis-born world historian, it is important to limit and define how 'conservatism' might be understood in the context of fourteenth-century North Africa. After all, this was the fractured political and social world that inspired Ibn Khaldun's most important writing. For the most part, conservatism seemed to mean returning to the models of the past, to the original vigor, be it mythical or actual, of the founders. As with Ibn Khaldun's renunciation of orange flowers, conservatism meant praising the morals and virtues of the countryside over the luxury and depravity of the city.

The various warring dynasties and rulers of fourteenth-century North Africa, the Hafsids, Marinids, Zayyanids and the Nasrids in Granada, divided and fought among themselves even as they formed alliances with rising Christian Mediterranean powers. Ibn Khaldun was a minister to all these powers. He faced the devastations of plague and pestilence in their cities, a pestilence that seemed divinely ordained. Conservatism was a return to the sources – not simply in religion but in social organization, a return to the virtuous simplicity of tribal life. After all, almost all the dynasties of North Africa as well as Granada, the last bastion of Islam in Spain, came from the countryside, from tribes outside of the city. The passages quoted at the beginning of this chapter seem to indicate that Ibn Khaldun's beliefs were in line with a classical definition of conservatism, the importance of long-accepted 'moral' standards, the martial prowess on 'group feeling' of natural groups, in his case the Bedouin and Berber tribes, and the need to respect the example and divine providence of the founding generation of any state or dynasty.

If conservatism meant advocating a return to the 'mythical founders' and a desire for stability, and a realist understanding of politics, and even faith (God favors the powerful over the weak dynasties), Ibn Khaldun seemed to be largely a conservative thinker. He had one historical dynasty in particular in mind: He regularly advocated a return to the spirit of the twelfth-century Almohad Empire. The Almohads, an example of success and power to whom he frequently alluded, served as a stable reference for Ibn Khaldun's unstable world. They established one of the first successful states in North African and Iberian history, but their power waned and they fractured into warring states and dynasties. The last Almohad Caliphs, increasingly dependent on Christian mercenaries sent from Spain, planted orange trees in Marrakech, encouraged cosmopolitanism and renounced the original Almohad doctrine born among the Berbers of the Atlas Mountains. To Ibn Khaldun, the Almohads, who once had great promise as rulers of an empire that could defeat the rising Christian tide in the West, fell victim to their own wealth and luxury. Ibn Khaldun also referred to the original, virtuous spirit of the Prophet Muhammad and the Rightly Caliphs, the first four successors of the Prophet: Abu Bakr, Umar, Uthman and 'Ali. But these beliefs in the inspired past as a model for the present were such a commonplace aspect of fourteenth-century writing that they are not so remarkable, and do not necessarily stand out. What was remarkable about Ibn Khaldun were his nuances, and his beliefs in new methods for understanding the past and human society. The case for Ibn Khaldun's conservatism is actually not as clear as it may at first seem. Was Ibn Khaldun largely conservative or was he actually progressive within a conservative age?

In fact, it has been argued that Christian, Jewish and Muslim scholars and thinkers of the medieval period from Maimonides to Averroes to Ibn Khaldun, hid their actual beliefs under a veil of conservatism. Although still the subject of raging controversy, this idea is associated with Leo Strauss and the Straussians of the University of Chicago, who tried to parse the 'true', deep beliefs of Maimonides from his political context. In this interpretation, outward conservatism was a survival tactic, a way of pleasing the ruler and avoiding rivals in claustrophobic, inquisitorial court cultures while remaining free to pursue philosophical ideas. One of the favorite means of deposing a rival wazir or minister was to accuse him of breaking conservative norms, or dabbling too much in the realm of heretical ideas. One could outwardly renounce challenges to the norm as a means of understanding them. But it was unclear to what degree Ibn Khaldun was 'forced' into conservatism in a Straussian way. An examination of his texts does not completely solve the mystery.

Ibn Khaldun, as the individual revealed in his writings, was almost as highly complex as he was highly educated. Ibn Khaldun left us with a rich corpus of writings, not only his famed *Muqaddimah*, or 'Introduction to History', quoted earlier, but also his *Autobiography*. From these texts, it seems clear that Ibn Khaldun not only had conflicting, even contradictory ideas, but also different personalities and perspectives that evolved over time. He really did seem to believe in the decline and fall of dynasties and power due to moral and social decadence. There was no indication in his writings that this stance was simply a ploy or an attempt to pull wool over the eyes of the rulers who sponsored him. In his position as minister of the tribes under Abu 'Inan in Fes and as ambassador to tribal groups under Abu al Abbas in Tunis, Ibn Khaldun had his own reasons to remind rulers of the importance of tribal power, which increased the importance of Ibn Khaldun's own political role. He was also once robbed of all his clothes by a mountain tribe and forced to roam naked through the hills until he finally found shelter. Only miraculous 'interventions from God' saved him.[4] This embrace of the tribes, even though he did recognize their dual ability to both found civilization and destroy it, sometimes landed Ibn Khaldun in trouble as a type of Cassandra who was too outspoken in warning about the consequences of inaction and the steps that were necessary to secure power – reaching out to the tribal groups on the margins of urban power. But while he condemned urban luxury and centralized education, and even, at times, Greek 'philosophy', Ibn Khaldun also seemed to know a great deal about education and Greek philosophy, and exhibited an encyclopedic range of other topics, listed exhaustively in his *Muqaddimah*. He also noted, uneasily, the rise of Western science. 'We further hear now that the philosophical sciences are greatly cultivated in the land of Rome and along the adjacent northern shore of the country of the European Christians.'[5]

While Ibn Khaldun's real attitude towards philosophical thinking may never be known, he clearly advocated a radical new way of thinking about history. Instead of simply relaying 'what happened' in a chronological approach with minimal analysis and respect for God's 'written book of fate', Ibn Khaldun sought 'the meaning behind events'. As a man of many contradictions, Ibn Khaldun was perhaps no different from other profound thinkers of different ages and places mentioned in this volume. His conservatism was contextual and his ideas, even those that seem explicitly conservative, were actually nuanced, betraying a certain 'progressive' tendency towards the study of history itself. He gave us the main reason for this new approach to history: the plague of 1348–49 CE (Ibn Khaldun, born in 1332, was in his teens at the time) that bore away almost every person he knew and destroyed familiar landmarks. The reason for the plague, according to Ibn Khaldun, was the 'dense and abundant civilization such as exists at the end of a dynasty'[6] Describing the plague, he wrote,

Their situation approached the point of annihilation and dissolution. Civilization decreased with the decrease of mankind. Cities and buildings were laid waste, roads and way signs were obliterated, settlements and mansions became empty, dynasties and tribes grew weak. The entire inhabited world changed ... It was as if the voice of existence in the world had called out for oblivion and restriction, and the world had responded to its call. God inherits the earth and whoever is upon it.[7]

Civilization and urban luxury, it seemed to Ibn Khaldun, were what killed his mother, his father, much of his family and friends and the old certainties of his youth. But, as it was to Boccaccio and other Mediterranean writers, the plague was also a key motivation of his writing. It sent Ibn Khaldun out on a search for meaning, a search to understand the brutalities of the world around him, a world that could not simply be the result of inscrutable, divinely ordained events in the book of God. Ibn Khaldun boldly dared to seek out the 'meaning behind events'. In doing so he challenged one of the most important conservative ideas of his era: the belief that, in time, God knows best. Yet it should not be assumed that Ibn Khaldun did not wish to play God, or he wished only to separate the affairs of man, subject as they were to greed, luxury and excess, from those of God. He did this by advocating a return to a mythical, original and pure understanding of human society, an idealization of the tribe and family ties and an idealization that restored some semblance of the world he lost to the plague.

Having lost confidence in the rulers of North Africa and Al-Andalus later in life, Ibn Khaldun went to Egypt. Tragically, his wife and children, who were sent on a separate ship, perished in a storm. Faced by yet more personal tragedy, his autobiography revealed snippets of his increasing sense of disillusion. Although he regularly was named Qadi, or head judge, of the Maliki, or mainly North African community in Egypt, a high role in Cairo society, he was also subject to frequent dismissal and the conniving of corrupt colleagues and rulers, the Mamluks, the 'slave rulers' of Egypt. Although he wished he could follow the example of his father, whom he idealized as embracing the 'spiritual life', he could not resist the allure of politics. He was regularly sent as an envoy for Mamluk interests.

In 1401 CE, in the last five years of life, Ibn Khaldun was secretly lowered in a basket, like St Paul, from the besieged walls of Damascus, one of the last bastions against Mongol power, to meet the terrible and infamous Timur the Lame (Timurlane). After showing deference to the great Sultan, Ibn Khaldun exclaimed rather cryptically, 'May God help you sir! It has been today thirty or forty years since I have hoped for this encounter.' Obviously puzzled and intrigued, since Ibn Khaldun could not have known about him so long ago, Timurlane asked, 'For what reason?'

'For two reasons', Ibn Khaldun responded, 'The first, is that you are the Sultan of the world, the King of the Earth; I have never known a king since the creation of Adam who is comparable to you.' Ibn Khaldun continued,

I do not base this observation on something out of thin air for I am a man of science ... Here is the explanation. Power does not exist without tribal solidarity ('asabiyya). Power is at its greatest extent among mainly tribal peoples, those whose lives are mostly governed by tribal solidarity. Men of science agreed on the fact that the two nations most tribal on earth are the Turks and the Arabs. You know of the great power of the Arabs after they were united by the religion of their prophet [Muhammad]. As far as the Turks, their [successful] rivalry against the Kings of Persia is sufficient witness to their power ... No King on earth, neither Chosroes, nor Caesar, nor Alexander nor Nebuchadnezzar had at their disposal a sense of tribal solidarity such as theirs.[8]

Scholars debate whether Ibn Khaldun really saw Timurlane, the great enemy of his Egyptian masters, who was also a major threat to the North African dynasties he once served, as the promised unifier of the Islamic world. He did not reveal his true opinions. Perhaps he was keeping his options open and protecting his life. Perhaps he was hoping for a man and a movement that might start a new, unified Islamic era.

Ibn Khaldun then gave the second reason for his mysterious foreknowledge of Timur's rise to power. Although dismissed by most modern scholars, I believe it was almost as interesting as his historical analysis: 'The divine predictions of the saints of North Africa: this was the second reason why I hoped I would see you.'[9] Ibn Khaldun saw no contradiction between his belief in the predictions of saints and the systemic and rational approach to historical analysis.

This conversation with Timur, as sincere or insincere it may have been, furnishes a clue to the nature of Ibn Khaldun's world view. Conservatism, for Ibn Khaldun, should not be blind. It was not only recognition of the patterns of the past, it was an embrace of radical change in pursuit of reviving that past and recognition of the mysterious nature of fate and events. In his old age, Ibn Khaldun sought to reconcile the two competing forces of his personality: a desire to understand the vagaries of this world with a resignation to the inscrutable forces of spirit and the divine. Ibn Khaldun was none other than the epitome of the traditional conservatism of his age; he was also its most radical opponent.

PART TWO

Modern moments

CHAPTER FOUR

Hume

James A. Harris

In all governments, there is a perpetual intestine struggle, open or secret, between AUTHORITY and LIBERTY; and neither of them can ever absolutely prevail in the contest. A great sacrifice of liberty must necessarily be made in every government; yet even the authority, which confines liberty, can never, and perhaps ought never, in any constitution, to become quite entire and uncontroulable. The sultan is master of the life and fortune of any individual; but will not be permitted to impose new taxes on his subject; a French monarch can impose taxes at pleasure; but would find it dangerous to attempt the lives and fortunes of individuals. Religion also, in most countries, is commonly found to be a very intractable principle; and other principles or prejudices frequently resist all the authority of the civil magistrate; whose power, being founded on opinion, can never subvert other opinions, equally rooted with that of his title to dominion. The government, which, in common appellation, receives the appellation of free, is that which admits of a partition of power among several members, whose united authority is no less, or is commonly greater than that of any monarch; but who, in the usual course of administration, must act by general and equal laws, that

*are previously known to all the members and to all their subjects.
In this sense, it must be owned, that liberty is the perfection of
civil society; but still authority must be acknowledged essential
to its very existence: and in those contests, which so often take
place between the one and the other, the latter may, on that
account, challenge the preference. Unless perhaps one may say
(and it may be said with some reason) that a circumstance, which
is essential to the existence of civil society, must always support
itself, and needs to be guarded with less jealousy, than one that
contributes only to its perfection, which the indolence of men is
so apt to neglect, or their ignorance to overlook.*[1]

This is the final paragraph of David Hume's essay 'Of the Origin of Government'. The essay appears to have been written in early 1774, two and a half years before Hume's death in August 1776. It was Hume's last contribution to political philosophy, indeed (as far as we know) his last new composition on any subject, and it is tempting therefore to read it as an attempt on Hume's part to summarize the principal lessons of his writings on politics. In so far as conservative thought places emphasis on the dangers of unbridled liberty and on the need for stable structures of authority, it is tempting also to read this essay as evidence that, by the end of his life, Hume situated himself in the conservative tradition. There is material for such an interpretation not only in the final paragraph, but in the main body of the essay as well, and especially in the doubt Hume expresses there about accounts of the origins of government and of the virtue of allegiance which are grounded in the rational pursuit of self-interest. 'Government', Hume claims, 'commences more casually and more imperfectly'.[2] The more psychologically realistic account offered by Hume instead is inspired by scepticism as to the human capacity for self-understanding and reflective foresight. It is implausible, Hume suggests, to imagine that human beings really did knowingly invent the duty of obedience to magistrates as a means of remedying the impossibility of keeping themselves in the paths of justice. More likely is the idea that the authority of one over the rest began in times of war, where courage and intelligence identified a particular individual as deserving obedience, and, as Hume puts it, 'where the pernicious effects of disorder are most sensibly felt'.[3] Because war was endemic to early human society, human beings became accustomed to submission, and the military chief's authority was gradually accepted in times of peace as well as times of war. The (sketchy) details of the later stages of the development of institutions of government are less important for present purposes than the general scepticism about the role of reason in history evinced by the account taken as a whole.

It seems likely that Hume wrote 'Of the Origin of Government' in response to contemporary political circumstances. On 16 December 1773, the 'Sons of Liberty' had boarded ships in Boston Harbour and thrown chests of tea into the water in protest against an Act of Parliament intended to force Britain's American colonies to pay duty on tea imported from the West Indies. In response, the British government passed a series of punitive laws, the Coercive Acts, which had the effect of intensifying American opposition to what was regarded as tyranny on the part of the Houses of Parliament. Hume's letters show that he took a keen interest in events in America, and that he was in favour of granting the colonies the independence they were demanding. His letters do not provide evidence, however, that he accepted the case the Americans themselves were making for a *right* to freedom from British domination. In Hume's eyes, the argument for American independence was pragmatic and economic. In essence, it was an argument that Britain would be better off if it let the colonies go than it would be if it tried, hopelessly, to hold on to them. This was, as John Pocock has noted, a Tory argument for a radical Whig conclusion.[4] Closer to home, and probably closer to the front of Hume's mind as he wrote this essay, there was the still-unresolved problem of John Wilkes. After five years as an outlaw in France following the threat of prosecution for seditious libel, Wilkes had been elected MP for Middlesex in 1768, only to be barred from taking his seat by a House of Commons that refused to have him as a member. Wilkes had then been twice re-elected to the Commons in ensuing by-elections, and expelled again each time afterwards. He was prevented also from running for Lord Mayor of London. The result was very serious unrest in London, and mass protests which on several occasions had to be put down with military force. The watchword of these protests was liberty, especially the liberty of the press to report on parliamentary debates, and also the more general issue of the right of the people to determine the membership of the House of Commons. In 1774, Wilkes finally overcame establishment opposition and was elected to and permitted to take up the position of Lord Mayor. Later in the same year he at last took up a seat in the House of Commons as a member for Middlesex.[5]

While Hume's letters are silent about the moral case for American independence, they are vociferous, in fact splenetic, in their hostility to the cause of 'Wilkes and Liberty'. They show that Hume was quite unable to see Wilkes and his supporters as making a serious and coherent case for political reform. Early on, in May 1768, Hume formed the opinion that 'these mutinies were founded on nothing, and had no connexion with any higher order of the state',[6] and he did not change his mind in the years that followed. He wrote to the French economist and statesman Turgot:

Here is a People thrown into Disorders (not dangerous ones, I hope) merely from the Abuse of Liberty, chiefly the Liberty of the Press; without any Grievance, I do not only say, real, but even imaginary; and without any of them being able to tell one Circumstance of Government which they wish to have corrected: They roar Liberty, tho' they have apparently more Liberty than any People in the World; a great deal more than they deserve; and perhaps more Liberty than any men ought to have.[7]

'This madness about Wilkes excited first Indignation, then Apprehension', he wrote to Hugh Blair in March 1769; 'but has gone to such a Height, that all other Sentiments with me are bury'd in Ridicule'. It was all more absurd even than the business of Titus Oates and the supposed 'Popish Plot' of 1678–81 that intended the assassination of Charles II so that he could be replaced by his openly Catholic brother James. Then there had been at least some explanation of popular frenzy, in the form of religion and the horror of Protestants at the idea of a Catholic monarch. But nothing could explain what was happening now. Religion, Hume told Blair, 'has, from uniform Prescription, acquir'd a Right to impose Nonsense on all Nations & all Ages: But the present Extravagance is peculiar to ourselves, and quite risible'.[8]

Hume's letters about Wilkes and Liberty have been read – notably by Giuseppe Giarrizzo[9] – as evidence of a conservative, authoritarian shift in his political thinking in the last phase of his philosophical career. It is not impossible to read 'Of the Origin of Government' also as the work of a cantankerous old man out of tune with the political ideas of the day. In the paragraph quoted earlier, Hume defines liberty as the division of power among the members of the government, and an obligation on the part of those members of government to 'act by general and equal laws, that are previously known to all the members and to all their subjects'. The Wilkites – and, of course, the Americans too – wanted more than that. They understood liberty to involve also some say on the part of subjects as to who some of the members of the government were, and thus a degree of influence over the character of a nation's laws. Hume, it could be claimed, is implicitly rejecting the liberty of self-government in 'Of the Origin of Government'. If so, however, this was no new departure in his political thought. On the contrary, it was merely a reiteration of a point he had made in his essays first published more than thirty years previously. In the essay 'Of Civil Liberty' (originally titled 'Of Liberty and Despotism'), Hume rejected the usual contrast between republics and monarchies, and claimed that 'in modern times' it could be said of 'civilized monarchies', such as France, '*that they are a government of Laws, not of Men*'. He explained: 'They are susceptible of order, method, and constancy, to a surprizing degree. Property is there secure; industry encouraged; the arts flourish; and the prince lives secure among his subjects, like a father among his children.'[10] This was not to say that in France there was no abuse of power, for example, in the way in which taxes were levied. But whatever imperfections there were in the French form of government were matched by imperfections in 'free governments' such as Britain: for example, the practice of contracting national debt without thought of its consequences for the future. This kind of challenge to received wisdom – eighteenth-century Britons prided themselves on the contrast between British liberty and French despotism – was from the beginning a key feature of what Duncan Forbes termed Hume's 'scientific', or 'philosophical', Whiggism.[11]

Another reason not to see 'Of the Origin of Government' as signalling a new turn in Hume's political thought is that the essay's scepticism about the role of reason in political history echoes a theme he had developed in earlier writings, most notably *The History of England* (1754–61). Hume the historian delights in the ironies of unintended consequences and the inability of even the most powerful men and women to determine the long-term effects of their actions. As Hume tells the story of the Reformation in England, nothing was further from Henry VIII's mind in 1529 than the creation of a Protestant church. And it was the religious fanaticism unleashed by the Reformation, not the efforts of Parliamentarians determined to preserve the rights enshrined in Magna Carta, that ultimately brought about the Glorious Revolution. The year 1688 is the *terminus ad quem* of *The History of England*, but in Hume's hands the creation of modern British liberty was, to use the language of 'Of the Origin of Government', both casual and imperfect. In his earliest discussion of political matters, the account of the obligation to allegiance in Book Three of *A Treatise of Human Nature*, Hume insinuated that the accession to the throne of William III was an act of violent usurpation.[12] In the essay 'Of the Original Contract', it was portrayed as a parliamentary coup.[13] Either way, here a further arguably conservative theme in Hume's political thought comes into view. For the question of to whom allegiance is due cannot, he argues, be settled by appeal to principles of reason. There are a number of rules that we naturally appeal to in order to decide that question, and it is perfectly possible for them to produce conflicting answers. This was the case in the immediate aftermath of 1688, when long possession spoke in favour of the Stuarts, and present possession, as well as positive law, spoke in favour of William. In the essay 'Of the Protestant Succession' Hume presented a scrupulously balanced account of the considerations that were in play as Parliament sought to decide whether or not permanently to exclude the Stuarts by passing the Act of Succession. The implication of the essay is that there was at that point no consideration that clearly settled the matter in favour of the House of Hanover. The key factor in political legitimation, Hume argued, is the passage of time.[14] The claim of the Stuarts was only permanently dismissed once enough time had passed for the Hanoverians to have, in the eyes of their subjects, sufficient authority to be obviously the protectors of the interests of the nation taken as a whole.

At the very end of 'Of the Origin of Government', Hume asserts that, while liberty may be the perfection of civil society, 'still authority must be acknowledged essential to its very existence'. The authority which Hume meant here, and about which he was always most concerned, was the authority of executive power. What was most important with respect to British politics was that the House of Commons did not acquire so much power at the expense of the Crown and its ministers that the executive was left unable to carry out the task of enforcing law and maintaining order. Only if a shift in the balance of power in favour of the Commons was prevented would the government taken as a whole be capable of performing its most essential role, which was to contain the intrinsically dangerous and destabilizing force that was 'the people'. Hume's letters of the late 1760s and early 1770s are dominated just as much by contempt at the inability of the Grafton and North ministries to master the situation as by revulsion at the actions of Wilkes and his supporters. 'Our Government has become an absolute Chimera,' Hume told William Strahan in October 1769: 'So much Liberty is incompatible with human Society.'[15] In a letter written in the summer of 1771 Hume listed the powers of government that had been lost since the accession of George III:

> The right of displacing the Judges was given up; General Warrants are lost; the right of Expulsion the same; all the co-ercive Powers of the House of Commons abandon'd; all Laws against Libels annihilated; the Authority of the Government impair'd by the Impunity granted to the Insolence of Beckford, Crosby, and the common Council: the revenue of the civil List diminishd. For God's sake, is there never to be a stop put to this inundation of the Rabble?[16]

An 'inundation of the rabble' was a permanent possibility in politics as Hume understood it. Government's first responsibility, a responsibility in respect of which it was currently failing, was to maintain the dykes that protected the country from flood. Hume's worry was that Britain was about to relive the nightmare of the 1640s and 1650s. He worried, in other words, that the granting of the liberties demanded by Wilkes and his followers would lead to anarchy, and that anarchy would be followed by what it was always followed by, tyranny.

Hume, it would seem, was unable to conceive of the people – those 'out of doors', who played no role in the business of government – as able to perform a positive, constructive function in British politics. The primary task of government was to protect the political community, and its property, from the rabble. Of course, opposition was by now an accepted feature of British politics. It was no longer another word for treason. But, as Hume saw it, opposition to a ministry's policies was legitimate only *inside* the Houses of Parliament. To Strahan in January 1770, Hume expressed the hope that the King's resolution to support the North ministry would henceforth be sufficiently obvious that 'men will either acquiesce or return to the ordinary, parliamentary Arts of Opposition'.[17] Extra-parliamentary opposition was by definition illegitimate and needed to be suppressed, by violent force if necessary.

'[T]he Audaciousness, Impudence, and Wickedness' of the City of London deserved punishment, Hume wrote in March 1770. Such punishment 'woud certainly produce a Fray; but what signifies a Fray, in comparison of losing all Authority to Government? There must necessarily be a Struggle between the Mob and the Constitution; and it cannot come at a more favourable time nor in a more favourable Cause'.[18]

There was nothing unusual in such sentiments in Britain at this time. It would be easy to find passages in Johnson, Walpole, Burke and many others, in which the sovereignty and inherent legitimacy of decisions of Parliament are affirmed in the same terms, and in which the growing weakness of the government is lamented just as bitterly. Here Hume's politics were not 'scientific' or 'philosophical', in Forbes's senses of the words, but instead very ordinary indeed.

Hume's response to the Wilkite movement reveals the essentially aristocratic character of his political thought. As David Miller (1981: 183) puts it, '[Hume]'s beliefs about government were formed on the underlying assumption that politics was an activity properly confined to a fairly select social group'.[19] This assumption – characteristic of conservatives, then and later – was always latent in his writings, but only in face of a movement of popular protest did Hume express it openly. It was an assumption that prevented him from being able, or even trying, to make sense of what was beginning to happen in England in the 1760s. For the new political movement headed by Wilkes could not, in truth, properly be described as the 1640s and 1650s come again. H. T. Dickinson and John Brewer have shown that the extra-parliamentary tactics adopted by Wilkes and his followers constituted a new departure in British politics.[20] The furore that followed the exercise by the House of Commons of its right to exclude a duly elected representative of the people – as we have seen, a right the eventual surrender of which Hume lamented – marked a significant shift in the country's political consciousness. According to Brewer, the controversy 'questioned the very basis on which a system of political stability had been built', because 'it questioned the grounds on which exclusion was justified, and because Wilkes and his supporters were adamant in their insistence that political power emanated from the *people*, and not from the oligarchical House of Commons'.[21] The Wilkes and Liberty affair thus brought into sharp relief the extent to which Hume accepted the common sense of his time about the people and their place, or rather their lack thereof, in the business of politics. Even so, and despite the other affinities noted here between Hume's political thinking and conservatism, Hume was not a conservative in the proper sense of the word, for there was, from his point of view, no serious and coherent radical ideology and no developed political philosophy advocating the comprehensive reform of existing political practices, from which the body politic needed to be protected.

CHAPTER FIVE

Edmund Burke (1729–97)

Mark Garnett

In this enlightened age I am bold enough to confess, that we are generally men of untaught feelings; that instead of casting away all our old prejudices, we cherish them to a very considerable degree, and, to take more shame to ourselves, we cherish them because they are prejudices; and the longer they have lasted, and the more generally they have prevailed, the more we cherish them. We are afraid to put men to live and trade each on his private stock of reason; because we suspect that this stock in each man is small, and that the individuals would be better to avail themselves of the general bank and capital of nations, and of ages. Many of our men of speculation, instead of exploding general prejudices, employ their sagacity to discover the latent wisdom which prevails in them. If they find what they seek, and they seldom fail, they think it more wise to continue the prejudice, with the reason involved, than to cast away the coat of prejudice, and to leave nothing but the naked reason; because prejudice, with its reason, has a motive to give action to that reason, and an affection which will give it permanence. Prejudice is of ready application in the emergency; it previously engages the mind in a steady course of wisdom and virtue, and does not leave the

man hesitating in a moment of decision, sceptical, puzzled, and
unresolved. Prejudice renders a man's virtue his habit; and not
a series of unconnected acts. Through just prejudice, his duty
becomes a part of his nature.[1]

Edmund Burke's claims for inclusion in the present volume are obvious; indeed, he is widely recognized as the founder of modern conservatism. Born and educated in Ireland, Burke abandoned the idea of following his father into the legal profession after migrating to London in 1750. Initially, he supported himself through writing, publishing *A Philosophical Enquiry into the Origin of Our Ideas of the Sublime and the Beautiful* in 1757 and becoming the founder-editor of the *Annual Register* in the following year. Always fascinated by politics, in 1765, he was appointed private secretary to the prime minister, Lord Rockingham, whose influence secured him a seat in the House of Commons. He remained an MP for almost 30 years, and served briefly as a junior government minister in the 1780s.

The problem of selection is unusually acute in Burke's case. The critic William Hazlitt – a vehement opponent of Burke's ideas – wrote after his death that 'to do him justice, it would be necessary to quote all his works; the only specimen of Burke is, all that he wrote'.[2] The excerpt chosen for this chapter comes from the predictable source – Burke's *Reflections on the Revolution in France* (1790), from which numerous passages could be selected. This one typifies the characteristic which makes the *Reflections* such a notable landmark in the history of conservative thought. Burke attacked the French Revolution – then in its early stages – both in theory and practice. Yet his account was not purely negative; the positive reasons Burke advanced for adhering to the status quo in France were founded on principles which could be applied in other countries (not least Britain itself). In short, through his defence of the pre-Revolutionary regime in France, Burke furnished something like a transnational manifesto for anyone who shared his general antipathy towards radical change.

As the excerpt suggests, Burke founded his case on a specific view of human nature. Tacitly, he drew a distinction between 'Men of speculation' and members of a community who, whether or not they enjoy direct political influence, do not endeavour to penetrate beneath the surface of events. Embracing without apology a word which even in Burke's day had strongly negative connotations – as Jane Austen confirmed in 1813 by twinning it with 'pride' – Burke argued that 'prejudice' was crucial to any functioning society. His notion of prejudice could, perhaps, have been given the more positive name of 'common sense'; it was a compound of intuition, folk memory and personal experience. This, he argued, is a far more reliable guide to action than abstract reason. In social interactions, it leads to a spontaneous preference for 'virtuous' conduct. In politics, it inspires profound respect for long-established institutions and practices. On close examination, political arrangements which seem unsupported by anything beyond unthinking 'prejudice' will almost invariably turn out to be susceptible to justification on rational grounds. Limited reforms will usually be sufficient to redress perceived abuses; in contrast, radical measures inspired by visions of political perfection are likely to make a tolerable situation much worse.

On the face of it, Burke's account could seem to have egalitarian implications. If prejudice is such a reliable guide, surely it must be safe to trust the general judgement of the people? However, Burke was a vehement opponent of democratic ideas, and spoke out against even modest proposals to reform the existing franchise in that direction. In the course of a 1782 speech on this subject, he had argued that 'The individual is foolish; the multitude, for the moment is foolish, when they act without deliberation; but the species is wise.'[3] This seems difficult to reconcile with the message of the *Reflections*, which implies that prejudice is good precisely because it prompts virtuous conduct without any need for 'deliberation'. Burke, though, would not have recognized any inconsistency. In his view, 'the bank and capital of nations, and of ages' suggested that political decisions should be entrusted to a suitably qualified elite. Thankfully, in Britain, there was a popular 'prejudice' in favour of this arrangement, which allowed ordinary people to go about their business without demanding greater influence in matters beyond their comprehension. At times of crisis, it may be proper for opinion-leaders – 'men of speculation' – to examine existing principles and practices. If the elite uses its influence responsibly, it will provide reassurance to 'the multitude', since, on inspection, it will discover the 'latent wisdom' which underpins the status quo. The real danger to society lies not in the prejudice in favour of deference, but rather in the possibility that 'men of speculation' will betray their privileged position by encouraging 'the multitude' to take independent action, or (still worse) to start speculating for themselves.

The ensuing debate showed that Burke had been right to identify the concept of 'prejudice' as a key line of division among commentators on the Revolution. In his reply to Burke, *The Rights of Man* (1791), Thomas Paine admitted that 'We have but a defective idea of what prejudice is.' But whatever it might be, it should be eradicated and replaced by 'opinion', which demanded rational reflection. 'No man', Paine wrote, 'is prejudiced in favour of a thing, knowing it to be wrong. He is attached to it in the belief that it is right; and when he sees it is not so, the prejudice will be gone.'[4] Paine thought that everyone should be sufficiently educated to be in a position to develop 'opinions', rather than relying on 'prejudice'. During the American Revolution, Burke and Paine had been allies of a kind, since Burke sympathized with the American rebels. But times had changed dramatically since then, and what Paine had considered to be 'common sense' when he wrote the influential pamphlet of that name (1775–76) seemed a recipe for murderous chaos to Edmund Burke of 1789. 'Common sense' and 'prejudice' might be value-laden words to denote what is essentially the same thing, but to the followers of Burke and Paine, they suggested entirely different responses to the political dilemmas of France after 1789. The Burkean view implies an overriding concern for social and political stability; Paine's ideas suggest a refusal to tolerate anything other than a dispensation which would win approval from a 'rational' observer. In short, responses to the debate between Burke and Paine over the value of 'prejudice' can be regarded as a key diagnostic test of 'conservatism' and liberalism to this day.

Burke's *Reflections* was a major publishing success even before the worst excesses of the French Revolution; when the French political classes started using the guillotine to settle their political scores, he could be hailed as an inspired prophet. This did not mean, however, that Burke was right in his diagnosis of the *causes* of the Revolution. As someone who attributed a central role in politics to ideas, it was not surprising that he was unduly harsh on French *philosophes*, notably Voltaire and Rousseau ('Atheists are not our preachers: madmen are not our lawgivers' [137]). It might be argued that Burke's exaggeration of the influence of ideas over the revolutionaries was an inspired mistake, since it provoked him into a systematic exposition of his own views. But it was not his only mistake; and in his state of overexcitement – which lasted from 1790 until his death seven years later – Burke laid himself open to lines of attack which have continued to be deployed against those who claim to be his legatees.

The most superficial, but nevertheless common, charge against Burke was one of inconsistency in his respective treatment of the American and French Revolutions. Burke, however, could reply that the American insurgents were defending their established practices against misguided British policy innovations. Nevertheless, it is possible that Burke's sharply contrasting responses to these major developments were affected by considerations relating to his own personal and political circumstances. In 1790, Burke was ageing and increasingly disenchanted with the leaders of his political party (the Whigs), notably Charles James Fox, who was an outspoken supporter of the French Revolution in its early stages. If the American and French Revolutions had occurred simultaneously in the 1770s, he might not have been so inclined to exercise empathy towards the one and vituperation towards the other.

More seriously, in his *Reflections*, Burke overstated his defence of the *Ancien Regime* in France, sometimes in ways which were painfully self-referential and romanticized. The most notorious example was his anecdote of meeting – or rather, glimpsing – the French Queen Marie-Antoinette. 'Surely never lighted on this orb, which she hardly seemed to touch, a more delightful vision,' he gushed in the *Reflections* (126). But even if this was an accurate recollection of the Queen's physical impact, it did not mean that the French people should tolerate monarchical misgovernment. Burke was running the familiar conservative risk, of sounding as if he was eulogizing the status quo and denying the efficacy even of limited reform. In fact, while critics (like Tom Paine) gleefully exploited this excruciating passage, Burke acknowledged that the *Ancien Regime* in France was far from perfect. Rather, he implied that it was amenable to improvement, through a series of reforms which could have brought it into proximity with the British system. To back this up, Burke offered a punchline: 'A state without the means of some change is without the means of its conservation' (72). During his own political career, he had tried to exemplify this maxim, particularly by urging the case for limited reforms which would reduce government expenditure. In fact, if implemented in full, Burke's proposals would have triggered a *radical* rebalancing of the British constitution as established by the 'Glorious Revolution' of 1688–89, by reducing the scope of monarchical influence over the political system as a whole. Equally, rather than being the unaided handiwork of malevolent ideologues, as Burke alleged, the French Revolution itself is better understood as a highly complex process which was instigated at least in part by well-meaning attempts at limited reform, which unwittingly released pent-up demands for more far-reaching changes.

In short, in a book which clearly delineated distinctively conservative principles, Burke had also contrived to underline the difficulties of applying them in *practice*. The ideology expounded in the *Reflections* implied a cautious approach to political questions, based on a sober evaluation of circumstances. Rather than self-consciously serving some ultimate political goal according to a predetermined blueprint, the Burkean conservative is engaged in a continuous process of piecemeal adaptation to unpredictable developments. The exercise of political *judgement* is thus essential to the conservative; and after the Revolution it became clear that Burke was now lacking in this quality. Embittered by his final separation from the Whigs, he lashed out at one of their number (the Duke of Bedford) in a *Letter to a Noble Lord* (1796) which could easily be read as a more general attack on the aristocratic element which, in a calmer context, Burke had regarded as essential to a stable sociopolitical order. It was as if Burke had spent so much time brooding about Rousseau, Voltaire et al. that he, too, had caught a dose of the 'French contagion'. The sensation aroused by the *Reflections* meant that Burke could not be ignored, even by his former political foe, Prime Minister William Pitt the Younger. Privately Pitt had dismissed the *Reflections* as 'rhapsodies ... in which there is much to admire and nothing to agree with'; he felt constrained to listen to Burke's advice on the conduct of the war against Revolutionary France, but resisted his demands for an explicitly pro-royalist policy.[5]

The society envisaged in the *Reflections* is unashamedly hierarchical, depending heavily on deference and an acute recognition of duties on the part of the privileged classes. While Burke's attack on Bedford implicitly conceded the obvious objection that aristocrats could sometimes be forgetful of their duties, other writings rejected the idea of obligations towards the poor. His *Thoughts and Details on Scarcity* (1795) – an attempt to influence Pitt's social policy, but not published until after Burke's death – decried any systematic attempt to alleviate distress, even when crops had failed due to inclement weather, making it difficult to apply the traditional distinction between 'deserving' and 'undeserving' objects of relief. Burke had formed the view that economic activity was governed by immutable laws, and expounded a free-market gospel with a zeal which made Adam Smith look like a socialist. It is just about possible to square this inflexible outlook with the philosophy of the *Reflections*, but only with considerable ingenuity. If the Laws of the Market really were heavenly decrees rather than the result of fallible human artifice, then it would indeed be imprudent to defy them. However, if their operation was threatening to cause mass starvation – or widespread social discontent, which presumably for Burke would be even more alarming – then their (partial) suspension might seem appropriate. This was precisely the approach adopted by William Pitt – himself a disciple of Adam Smith, who advocated relief of the poor on the grounds that abstract principles, however impressive on paper, should be overridden in 'unexpected situations'.[6]

In the *Reflections*, Burke lamented that 'the age of chivalry is gone. – That of sophisters, oeconomists and calculators, has succeeded' (126). His inability to budge from abstract theory on the question of poor relief places him firmly on the side of the 'oeconomists and calculators'. Burke's position also jars against his exalted view of the state, which 'ought not to be considered as nothing better than a partnership agreement in a trade of pepper and coffee, calico or tobacco, or some other such low concern', but rather 'a partnership in all science; a partnership in all art; a partnership in every virtue, and in all perfection' (147). He might have predicted the blood-soaked course of the French Revolution with remarkable accuracy, but did not detect the developments in industrial processes which were already beginning to trigger a different kind of 'revolution' in Britain itself. In time, this would raise serious questions about the relevance of Burke's assumptions about the nature of society, as well as exposing the fault line between his distinctively conservative take on human reason and his economic theorizing. While a failure to anticipate the full sociopolitical impact of industrialization is forgivable, having served as MP for the port city of Bristol between 1774 and 1780, Burke had an excellent vantage-point from which to identify the incompatibility between attitudes based on the desire for unlimited accumulation and the outlook of the rural aristocracy, exemplified by so many of his parliamentary colleagues. As such, Burke's simultaneous championship of a conservative world in the *Reflections*, and of the economic ideas which were likely to destroy it, was a symptom of something more than an intellectual blind spot.

Although Burke had always seen himself as a Whig, his eloquent opposition to radical change earned him recognition as a spiritual inspiration for the Conservative Party, when the Tories adopted that name in 1834.

However, in reputation as in life William Pitt was regarded as a far more important role model.[7] Even the change of nomenclature suggested that Burke's conservative ideas, and their embodiment in British institutions, were threatened with redundancy; at least in part, the Tories of 1834 chose a more explicit ideological label in order to rededicate themselves to the increasingly onerous and thankless task of 'conserving' some familiar political landmarks in the face of overwhelming challenges. The most obvious danger was the end of aristocratic dominance of political activity, thanks mainly to the 1832 Reform Act. Burke himself had been a champion of representative institutions, but regarded anything approaching universal (manhood) suffrage as the harbinger of mob rule. While the Conservatives continued to advertise themselves as an indispensible source of stability, in practice they could only try to live up to this role by presiding over (and occasionally even promoting) institutional changes which made Britain an essentially *liberal* state, opening the party to accusations of 'opportunism' (particularly under Benjamin Disraeli).

Arguably, by the twentieth century, the only vestige of 'Burkean' influence on the Conservative Party was its sporadic expressions of veneration for its own traditions and for 'founding fathers' like Burke, although even these displays began to take on the appearance of empty rituals. Burke could be made to seem relevant to new challenges to the status quo in Britain and abroad after the 1917 Bolshevik Revolution; after all, few people had issued more potent warnings about the effects of radical change of any kind. Yet his message was at best ambiguous in this new context, and even positively unhelpful to anti-socialists who noticed his lyrical evocation of the state. Burke's *Reflections*, after all, had been a diatribe against *liberal* ideologues; yet in 1917, the most determined opposition to 'Bolshevism' came from Western governments whose habitual mode of thought in the new age of democracy bore more than a passing resemblance to those of the 'execrable philosophers' whom Burke held responsible for the atrocities in France after 1789.

Under the Conservative Party leader David Cameron (2005–16), Burke suddenly became the focus of more practical interest as a partial inspiration for the idea of the 'Big Society' – essentially an attempt to remind citizens that some state functions could be carried out more effectively (and at less expense to taxpayers) by voluntary organizations.[8] Burke could certainly be cited as an advocate of 'civil society', and as so often had bequeathed to the campaign a useful sound bite in his reference in the *Reflections* to 'the little platoon(s) we belong to in society' (97). Again, however, the appeal to Burke threatened to raise awkward (indeed unanswerable) questions at the level of practical decision-making. In particular, Burke saw membership of the 'little platoon' as 'the first link in a series by which we proceed towards a love to our country and to mankind'. The fact that Cameron felt it necessary to 'nudge' Britons towards community action suggests a recognition that atomized liberal individualism – encouraged most notably by his own

Conservative predecessor, Margaret Thatcher (see Chapter 16) – had broken the first link in Burke's beneficent 'series'.

In summary, Edmund Burke deserves to be recognized as a major (perhaps even the greatest) exponent of conservative philosophy. That is, his argument against radical change can be distilled into a coherent approach to political questions, based ultimately on a view of human nature which explains why such changes are likely to result in catastrophe, while underpinning a much more positive case for gradualism. However, while William Hazlitt was justified in his assertion that Burke could not be appreciated in full without reading 'all that he wrote', a comprehensive survey of that kind reveals enduring dilemmas for people who, since Burke's day, have regarded themselves as 'conservatives'. Even during his lifetime, it was possible to identify some elements of his thinking which could not easily be reconciled with the 'distilled' version; in particular, as we have seen, his economic ideas were ill chosen for a politician with an overriding preoccupation with social and institutional stability. In this respect, one can at least claim that Burke's 'conservative' successors (whether 'thinkers' or 'practitioners') have fared no better, and with less excuse, in their attempts to square these circles.

CHAPTER SIX

Alexander Hamilton

Michael P. Federici

There are some who would be inclined to regard the servile pliancy of the Executive to a prevailing current, either in the community or in the legislature, as its best recommendation. But such men entertain very crude notions, as well of the purposes for which government was instituted, as of the true means by which the public happiness may be promoted. The republican principle demands that the deliberate sense of the community should govern the conduct of those to whom they intrust the management of their affairs; but it does not require an unqualified complaisance to every sudden breeze of passion, or to every transient impulse which the people may receive from the arts of men, who flatter their prejudices to betray their interests. It is a just observation, that the people commonly INTEND the PUBLIC GOOD. This often applies to their very errors. But their good sense would despise the adulator who should pretend that they always REASON RIGHT about the MEANS of promoting it. They know from experience that they sometimes err; and the wonder is that they so seldom err as they do, beset, as they continually are, by the wiles of parasites and sycophants, by the snares of the ambitious, the avaricious, the desperate, by the artifices of

men who possess their confidence more than they deserve it,
and of those who seek to possess rather than to deserve it.
When occasions present themselves, in which the interests of the
people are at variance with their inclinations, it is the duty of the
persons whom they have appointed to be the guardians of those
interests, to withstand the temporary delusion, in order to give
them time and opportunity for more cool and sedate reflection.
Instances might be cited in which a conduct of this kind has saved
the people from very fatal consequences of their own mistakes,
and has procured lasting monuments of their gratitude to the men
who had courage and magnanimity enough to serve them at the
peril of their displeasure.[1]

Alexander Hamilton has achieved an improbable feat for any reputed conservative: more than two centuries after his death, his biography has inspired a hit Broadway musical. It celebrates the rise of an extraordinarily talented and ambitious man who did as much as any American to win independence, create a constitutional republic and build economic and political institutions that would last for centuries.

Hamilton was born out of wedlock on the island of Nevis in the British West Indies in 1755 to Rachel Faucette and James Hamilton. Hamilton's father left the family when Alexander was ten, and his mother died when he was twelve. After their mother's death, he and his brother James were disinherited and placed in the care of a cousin, Peter Lytton, who committed suicide shortly after the Hamilton boys arrived at his home. Having to make his own way, Hamilton worked for Nicholas Cruger and David Beekman, two New York merchants who soon recognized Hamilton's extraordinary talent for finance, organization and leadership, three characteristics that would be apparent throughout his life.

Cruger and a local minister, Hugh Knox, arranged for Hamilton to travel to the American colonies and attend college. After a year's study at Elizabethtown Academy in New Jersey to prepare for college entrance exams, Hamilton was admitted to King's College (Columbia University) and nearly completed his studies before enlisting in the Continental militia as an artillery captain. He distinguished himself in battle and preparation of his troops and was asked to join George Washington's staff, where he served for years as Washington's aide-de-camp. Subsequently, he commanded a New York light-infantry battalion, winning acclaim for his leadership at the Battle of Yorktown. Hamilton passed the bar in New York, was a highly respected and sought-after attorney and served in the state legislature and the Confederate Congress. He attended the Annapolis and

Philadelphia conventions and wrote two-thirds of the *Federalist Papers* (1787–88). Selected by Washington to be the first secretary of the treasury, he created a banking and currency system, an assumption plan that would transfer state war debt to the national government, the customs service, and wrote influential reports on manufacturing and public credit. After serving as secretary of the treasury, he continued to influence American politics and lead the Federalist Party. He served as solicitor general in the John Adams administration. He died in 1804 after being shot in a duel with Vice President Aaron Burr.

The passage provided earlier captures the core of Hamilton's political thinking and the generally conservative nature of his political theory and statesmanship. What stand out in the passage from *Federalist* 71 and in Hamilton's political theory as conservative are three things: Hamilton's views of human nature, democracy and leadership. Hamilton was a moral dualist in his view of human nature and less inclined towards democracy than just about any American founder. He was also an advocate of natural aristocracy, a class of elites who were qualified for positions of leadership not by birth or wealth, but by talent and ability. Hamilton was himself able to rise to the upper ranks of America's ruling class even though he came from such humble beginnings because, unlike European nations of the time, the United States opened its ruling class to a broader range of individuals although it excluded women and African Americans.

In *Federalist* 71, Hamilton defends an independent executive and articulates an important part of his republican theory, what today might be called a theory of democracy. In his day, Hamilton was a republican not a democrat, an important distinction then and now. In the late eighteenth century, 'democracy' was considered something akin to direct or pure democracy. In a pure democracy, there are no representatives and the people rule directly, outside the framework of constitutional checks and balances and the separation of powers. It assumes the infallibility or near-infallibility of the people, based on their natural goodness. Elites, by contrast, are assumed to be corrupt and incapable of promoting the true interest of the people. On this theory, the objective of government is to allow the direct will of the people to guide society. The American Framers, including Hamilton, were at odds with democracy because it led to disorder, if not anarchy, it was incapable of controlling factions and it was susceptible to demagogues.

Hamilton's political theory is grounded in a conservative prejudice regarding human nature, leadership and the possibilities of politics. In this view, human beings of all classes are imperfect and imperfectable. Consequently, government is necessary to control the passions of individuals who are prone to follow mere self-interest and demagogues who flatter them to acquire power rather than to serve the public good. Popular government is possible, but not in the form of pure democracy; it requires both institutions and leaders of character for it to comport with the higher aspirations of politics and civilization such as justice and the common good.

Representatives of exceptional character are needed to filter the public will through an elaborate constitutional system of separated powers and checks and balances. Were the people's voice the voice of God, as some claimed, such checks and restraints would be unnecessary, but taking human nature for what it has been historically, Hamilton was intent on building political institutions that would frustrate the immediate passions of 'the people' when they undermined the public good. The people are no different from individuals in that both are apt to succumb to lower appetites in the passion of the moment. They tend to be at their best and most apt to discover the public good when they have time to deliberate, reflect, and compromise. While Hamilton placed a higher degree of trust in a ruling elite than the people, he was well aware that rulers and the people alike possessed the same flawed human nature and needed to be checked and restrained. Such restraints were provided by the character of leaders and the institutional checks and limits on power that define the essence of constitutional government, including popular checks such as elections.

In this way, Hamilton was like the eighteenth-century British statesman and thinker Edmund Burke. The independent judgement of representatives was vital to good government because they were more likely than the people to be in the habit of subordinating individual interest to the common good. To Hamilton's thinking, the people were prone to follow the wiles of demagogues and sycophants and engage in self-interested factions that undermined the common good. He viewed domestic insurrections such as Shays's Rebellion, the Whiskey Rebellion and Fries Rebellion in this light. Hamilton did, however, see a role for the people in constitutional government. He supported a popular house of Congress elected directly by the people that would express the people's will, but it needed to be checked by an upper house and a president that were more permanent in that they served life terms and were aristocratic in character.

Hamilton distinguished between 'true politicians' and 'political empyrics'.[2] The former were individuals who possessed republican virtue, a moral standard originating in Roman times which demanded that they should rise above mere self-interest and promote the greater good. The latter were all too common in republics. They lacked republican virtue and could disguise their self-serving ambitions behind demagogic flattery. The way to minimize the influence of such pernicious leaders was to rely on an aristocratic class of true politicians and constitutional institutions that provided checks and restraints on popular will. George Washington exemplified the true politician. He was a model of republican virtue and a man of high character.

When Hamilton defended Washington's neutrality proclamation of 1793 writing as 'Pacificus', he was applying the political ideas articulated in *Federalist* 71. While Jeffersonians insisted that the United States was obligated by treaty and common ideology to enter the French Revolutionary Wars on the side of France, Hamilton supported Washington's decision to remain neutral and he rejected the notion that the French revolutionaries shared the principles of American republicanism. Moreover, Hamilton insisted that it was the president's prerogative and not Congress's to create a policy of neutrality. Better to have the president who is vested with all executive power and the sole representative of the nation exercise his judgement than to place all discretion in one branch, the legislature. The executive needs to be independent of the legislature and the people. What gives the president such independent judgement? Institutionally, he is not elected directly by the people but by the electoral college; he has veto power over the Congress, and he was originally not subject to term limits. Hamilton advocated a life term for the president at the Constitutional Convention in 1787, but there was little support for his position. He believed that a life term combined with the other institutional characteristics of the presidency would give the office what he called 'permanence' and 'energy'.[3]

It is apparent that Hamilton's political theory is at odds with at least part of the liberal tradition. Unlike Rousseau, he does not elevate the will of the people to paramount sovereignty. In Rousseau's social contract theory, the general will is the unfiltered momentary will of the people uncorrupted by conventions and reflection. It stems from the natural goodness of human beings and thus is the measure of justice and good. Hamilton's insistence on a deliberate will that is the product of 'cool and sedate reflection' is contrary to Rousseau's notions of man's natural goodness and the general will. Moreover, contrary to both Rousseau and Locke, Hamilton does not subordinate executive power to legislative power. He insists that it be independent of the legislative branch and the people. While Hobbes argues for a strong executive, his 'Leviathan' is different from Hamilton's executive in both degree and kind. Hamilton's executive exists within the structure of separated powers and checks and balances. Hobbes's Leviathan operates outside such restraints and holds absolute power. Hamilton's view of human nature does not support pure government of any type that places all power in the hands of one person, one branch of government, or the people. Contrary to the social contract theorists, he thus favored a mixed republic that combined elements of monarchy, aristocracy and democracy.

The structural/institutional differences between Hamilton and social contract thinkers stem from competing conceptions of human nature and politics. Hobbes, Locke and Rousseau consider humans to be more rational than does Hamilton. Hamilton is more sceptical about the ethical and rational nature of humans. He argued that 'Men are rather reasoning tha[n] reasonable animals for the most part governed by the impulse of passion.'[4] Social contract theory assumes humans to be sufficiently rational to leave the state of nature, form a social contract and, in some cases, engage in revolution when government violates the contract. The notion, readily apparent in Hamilton's political thinking, that revolution and insurrection bring out the worst as well as the best in many individuals, gives reason to be sceptical about the fortunes of individuals when they engage in violent revolution. Revolution creates a habit of anarchy and resistance to authority that may be justified at times, but it is difficult to control once left to run wild in the circumstances of revolution. Hamilton identified such temperament in the Sons of Liberty, a vigilante group created to harass and terrorize Loyalists and resist the Stamp Act on the eve of the War for Independence.

Like Burke, Hamilton trusted the wisdom of experience and was essentially Christian in his view of human nature. As a consequence, Hamilton was sober about the possibilities of politics and suspicious of political movements, like Jacobinism, that were irreligious. While both thinkers were keen to emphasize the limits of politics and considered it the art of the possible, they were steadfast reformers. It was revolution, insurrection and radical change that they opposed for the same reasons that Hamilton rejected pure democracy; that is, human beings are especially prone to vice and the will to power when inflamed by the passion of the moment. Both were adamantly opposed to the French Revolution, but favorably disposed to American independence. Both were also opponents of slavery and offered reforms to destroy it. They were generally in favor of free markets, but did not place the value of economic freedom above all else. Burke and Hamilton were sensitive to the effect of corruption in government. A class of natural aristocrats was necessary for the government to function properly, and corruption undermined the legitimacy of honest rulers who promoted the public good. In foreign affairs, they were steadfast in supporting their nation, but cautious about overreaching. Both sensed that too much attention to distant lands would adversely affect the polity at home. Both men had a flair for oratory and could carry a debate for hours at a time. Both elicited the wrath of radicals intent on the transformation of human beings and society. Both were strident anti-Jacobins. In sum, both Burke and Hamilton were consistent with the traditional understanding of conservatism, in that they advocated prudent reform and opposed revolutionary change. Tradition informed by historical experience was their guide in differentiating between prudent reform and misguided idealism.

Contemporary conservatives tend to be divided on Hamilton. More libertarian and localist conservatives see him as the father of big government, mass society and American nationalism. Hamilton was at the forefront in the generation of American Founders arguing for a stronger national government. As the Constitution was implemented, Hamilton's policies made the idea of a stronger national government a reality. His banking and currency systems, tax policies, customs service, advocacy for a standing and well-funded army, loose construction of the Constitution and positive view of bureaucracy were, to some, ingredients for a counter-revolution that transformed the new nation from a decentralized agricultural republic to a large, centralized manufacturing-based commercial republic. Other conservatives, however, view Hamilton in a more favorable light. They see him as the defender of order and meritocracy. Hamilton's sober view of human nature and politics appeals to these more traditional conservatives who applaud his role in creating the Constitution and opposing the French Revolution. They also appreciate Hamilton's warnings against foreign entanglements and support for Washington's Neutrality Proclamation. His arguments about the shortfalls of democracy also find sympathy among traditional conservatives.

Hamilton's relevance to contemporary American politics is difficult to gauge. For decades, conservatives and liberals have taken an array of positions on Hamilton's political and economic theories as well as his statesmanship. Supporters and opponents can be found on all sides of the ideological spectrum, and it is evident that the circumstances of contemporary American politics have changed dramatically from the late eighteenth century. Were he alive today, would Hamilton support the welfare state and global American empire? Such questions, to be useful, need to be reformulated. We might ask whether contemporary American politics can be supported or opposed on Hamiltonian grounds. A few issues are worth considering. It is difficult to reconcile America's role in the world since the First World War with the ideas that Hamilton and Washington articulated in the 1796 Farewell Address. While Hamilton favored a standing army that was well equipped, he did not believe that any one form of government was best for all nations, nor should nations use military force to impose their political system on other cultures. Hamilton's opposition to the French Revolution and the Jacobin efforts to spread its radical ideology globally suggest that any movement that aims at global democracy is un-Hamiltonian. Likewise, while the progressive movement in the United States has some similarity to Hamilton's support for a strong and energetic executive, his political theory is at odds with much of progressivism. For one, its idealistic view of human nature and politics is contrary to Hamilton's philosophical anthropology. He was not inclined to use the power of government for the purpose of transforming human nature or building utopias, nor can Hamilton's view of presidential power serve as a justification for a unitary executive that exercises power outside the confines of constitutional checks and balances and the separation of powers. Hamilton faced an intellectual environment that tended to favor legislative power. The Articles of Confederation created a one-branch legislative government. At the Constitutional Convention in 1787, Hamilton opposed both the Virginia and New Jersey Plans precisely because they gave too much power to the legislative branch and too little power to the executive. His plan, often maligned as an attempt to create an American monarchy, was intended to pull the delegates away from legislative supremacy and toward a strong, independent executive. His success in this matter is underestimated and underappreciated.

In short, there is little about the character of contemporary American politics that resembles Hamilton's politics. Both liberals and conservatives have embraced an immodest scale of government in both domestic and foreign affairs that compels the federal government to run deficits that Hamilton would likely consider irresponsible. While Hamilton supported the idea of public debt, he insisted on the need to manage it well, meaning that when necessary it might increase, but when possible it would be reduced so as not to burden the federal budget unnecessarily. Hamilton was also an advocate of building the nation's infrastructure and the manufacturing sector of the economy. Both have been neglected in recent decades as Americans have been encouraged to borrow beyond their means and spend in excess, much of it on cheap foreign goods. Some have suggested that Hamilton's view of constitutional interpretation has become the dominant approach on the Supreme Court. Such comparisons take a superficial similarity regarding how strictly one interprets that Constitution and ignores important differences. Hamilton explicitly states in *The Federalist* that federal judges should not make law and that they should be impeached for doing so. Having underestimated the potential of the judiciary to exceed its constitutional power, he expected the other branches of government, especially Congress, to guard their power against judicial encroachments. Hamilton argued for 'a reasonable construction' of the Constitution which meant that general grants of constitutional power, specified in the Constitution, provide government with discretion to use a variety of unenumerated means to promote the legitimate ends of government.[5] Though his economic policies increased the size and scope of the national government, Hamilton lived during a time when the immediate need was to correct the weakness of government under the Articles of Confederation. The development of American politics into an imperial war state abroad and welfare state at home owes less to Hamilton than to the progressives of the twentieth century such as Woodrow Wilson, Franklin Roosevelt and George W. Bush.

CHAPTER SEVEN

Samuel Taylor Coleridge

John Morrow

The positive ends [of government] are, 1st to make the means of subsistence more easy to each individual: 2d. that ... he should derive from the union and division of labour a share of the comforts and conveniences, which humanize and ennoble his nature; and at the same time the power of perfecting himself in his own branch of industry ... 3dly. The hope of bettering his own condition and that of his children. . . . (and lastly) the development of those faculties which are essential to his human nature by the knowledge of his moral and religious duties, and the increase of his intellectual powers ... [T]hat Constitution is the best, under which the average sum of useful knowledge is the greatest, and the causes that awaken and encourage talent and genius, the most powerful and various.[1]

[A] Constitution is an idea arising out of the idea of a state; and because our whole history from Alfred onwards demonstrates the continued influence of such an idea, or ultimate aim, on the minds of our fore-fathers, ... we speak ... of the idea itself, as actually existing, i.e., as a principle, ... in the minds and consciences of the persons, whose duty it prescribes, and whose rights it determines. (19)[2]

[I]n every country of civilised men, acknowledging the rights of
property ... the two antagonistic powers of opposite interest in
the state, under which all other state interests are comprised, are
those of PERMANENCE and of PROGRESSION. (24)
... In order to correct views respecting the constitution, in a more
enlarged sense of the term, viz. the constitution of the Nation, we
must, in addition to a grounded knowledge of the State, have the
right idea of the National Church. *These are the two poles of the*
same magnet; the magnet itself, which is constituted by them, is
the CONSTITUTION of the nation. (31)

Samuel Taylor Coleridge's *On the Constitution of the Church and State*
(1830) was the last significant work of a philosophically informed poet
and man of letters whose political oeuvre included a range of pamphlets,
substantial essays and slighter journalistic pieces. Coleridge's earliest
political publications were products of a period in the mid-1790s when his
ideas intersected at a number of points with those of radical political and
religious reformers that posed a sharply felt challenge to the fundamentally
conservative Anglican 'church-state' of eighteenth-century Britain. The
references to historical continuity and ancestry, property and the 'National
Church' in the extracts mentioned at the beginning of this chapter suggest
that Coleridge's political ideas had undergone a markedly conservative shift
over the course of his adult life. His late conservatism, however, retained
distinctive critical and progressive elements.

In political as well as in literary criticism, Coleridge revelled in
terminological distinctions which implicitly qualified more conventional
usages. Thus, in *Church and State*, he sometimes uses the terms 'state' and
'commonwealth' to refer to political communities in the broadest sense,
but he also drew a distinction between the 'constitution of the state' and
the 'constitution of the nation'. The former referred to the legislative and
executive arms of government, while the latter set these within a more
extensive institutional framework which included the 'national church'. The
discussion focused on the historical practice of British government but that
was regarded as a particular instance of more general principles of politics
and morals.

Coleridge's mature political theory was underwritten by two fundamental
sets of assumptions about politics and the state. The first concerned the
moral and political significance of property, while the second charged the
government with distinctive material and moral responsibilities. Coleridge
regarded private property as a means through which humans could give
practical expression to their God-given endowment of free will, the faculty

through which they 'intuitively know the sublimity, and the infinite hopes, fears, and capabilities of [their] own nature.'[3] Moreover, he claimed that where private property existed, it should determine the distribution of political power within a political community or state: 'that *Government is good in which property is secure and circulates; that Government the best, which, in the exactest ration, makes each man's power proportionate to his property*'.[4] Coleridge insisted there should be no 'direct political power without cognizable possession', no direct access to the organized powers of the state without those 'fastening and radical fibres of a collective and registerable property, by which the Citizen inheres in and belongs to the Commonwealth' (87–8). In writings dating from 1799 to 1800, he had underlined the importance of this requirement by identifying the dangers inherent in a new French constitution ushered in under the auspices of Napoleon Bonaparte, whose dominant position in French politics was due to his control of the army. Coleridge was highly critical of the constitution of 1799 because the absence of property qualifications for members of the legislative body meant that they would be entirely dependent on the executive for their livelihood and particularly susceptible to his or her wishes.[5] Their political interest as proprietors was derived from a government based on military strength rather than from their standing as independent members of the community. The understanding of the relationship between property and political power that underwrote Coleridge's mature political theory derived from the seventeenth-century republican thinker, James Harrington, who had promoted republican government on the grounds that it reflected shifts in the distribution of landed property as England moved away from feudalism. While Coleridge adopted this general line of reasoning, however, he applied it also to new forms of wealth derived from 'commerce' that had become significant since Harrington's time.

In eighteenth- and early-nineteenth-century Britain, the 'landed interest' was a widely understood shorthand for an elite made up of members of the aristocracy, and 'country gentlemen', or 'gentry'. The political power of the landed interest was focussed in the House of Lords and in seats in the lower house and reflected in its leading role in the executive arm of government. Its political influence in the 'constitution of the state' was underwritten by territorial domination that made it a powerful economic and social force in the country areas and provincial towns where its estates were located. In many ways, Coleridge's understanding of the landed interest mirrored conventional 'Tory' accounts that stressed the values of a traditional society, identified it with the historical transmission of values and property, habits of ingrained deference, a predisposition to seek psychological comfort in traditional practices and ideas and a commitment to the social duties customarily attached to land ownership. References to the landed classes as the 'permanent' interest epitomized its attachment to tradition and aversion to change. They also, however, signalled the close and distinctive relationship which he thought existed between land ownership and fundamental moral values.

Coleridge's views on the moral implications of land ownership emerged in 1799–1816 as he distanced himself from the anti-establishment radicalism of the mid-1790s. In *The Friend*, which appeared originally in 1809–10 and was reissued in 1816, and in *Lay Sermons* of 1816–17, he argued that because agricultural activity was necessary to sustain life and hence the communities to which humans naturally belonged, the ownership of the land involved distinctive obligations and privileges. In hierarchical societies such as Britain, where property holdings were very unequal, the privileges of land ownership meant that it was to be regarded as being held as a trust conditioned by the ends of the state.[6] The landed classes were thus obliged to take account of the material needs of their dependents, contribute to their capacity to improve their condition and that of their children and assist them to secure the guidance and education necessary to foster the development of their potentialities for rationality and morality.

In Britain, and to a lesser extent in other European countries, the interests of permanence coexisted with progressive impulses springing from commercial, mercantile and industrial property. Drawing on eighteenth-century theories of 'commercial society', Coleridge identified 'commerce' with free-market activity and attributed to it the growth of society's productive capacity and the prosperity and influence of those who engaged successfully in it. These features of commercial society were of great positive significance for the advancement of the first three ends of the state. Increased productivity and the circulation of property beyond the confines of landed society, extending potentially at least into the peasantry and urban working classes, provided enhanced opportunities for moral development by broadening the scope for free agency, as well as improving the quality of material life of all members of the community. In addition, however, Coleridge endorsed the widely held view that commercial societies fostered the progressive advance of 'civilisation', through the refinement of 'manners' and the spread of the civilities of 'polite' society, the extension of the 'rights and privileges of citizens' to wider sections of the community, and the development of the arts, practical knowledge and public information (25). But while Coleridge acknowledged that commerce might make valuable contributions to advancing the first three positive ends of the state, he noted that its ethos was quite different from that arising from landed property and would not contribute to the advancement of the fourth educational and moral objective: 'To introduce any other principle ... but that of obtaining the highest price with adequate security for Articles fairly described, would be tantamount to the position, that Trade ought not to exist.'[7]

Coleridge's understanding of the characteristics and implications of landed and commercial property provided the basis for his distinctive reworking of the conventional idea that the British constitution was efficacious because it maintained a balance between the upper and lower house and between these houses and the Crown. This arrangement was usually expressed in the idea that sovereign power rested with 'the king in parliament'. By contrast, Coleridge's account focused on the implications of a constitutional structure that balanced the interests of permanence and progression rather than on the relationship between the formal elements of the constitution. He thus pointed out that while the growth of commercial wealth was reflected in the changing membership of the house of commons, it had been productively integrated in the 'constitution of the state' by the ongoing influence of countervailing tendencies emanating from the landed classes in the lower and upper houses of parliament. Coleridge described these interests as being in a condition of balance or 'equipoise' and characterized this relationship by an electromagnetic analogy that eschewed the mechanical images usually applied to the relationship among various formal elements of the constitution. He described these interests as 'opposites', rather than 'contraries', and saw them as the source of an invigorating unified force analogous to that arising from the negative and positive poles of a magnet (24n). The Crown's role in assenting to legislation expressed 'the majesty, or symbolic unity of the whole nation, both of the state and the persons' (41–2). Significantly, Coleridge did not believe that the Crown's role was to check or balance the proprietorial interests reflected in the legislature.

Although Coleridge's account of the 'constitution of the state' reflected a particular understanding of the history and practice of the British constitution, it was underpinned by a general theory of legitimate government. This theory incorporated ideas about the direct relationship between property rights and political power and the ends of the state. His analysis showed how the political forces generated by radically different forms of property might be brought into a relationship that maintained the benefits associated with traditional attitudes, practices and values while harnessing the progressive material and social possibilities unleashed by the spirit of commerce. As signalled in the last part of the head quote, however, Coleridge insisted that the balance of interests that made up the 'constitution of the state' had to be seen as but part of a more extensive 'constitution of the nation'. It was only within this enlarged constitutional structure that political communities were able to realize the goals of government and form a genuine commonwealth.

Coleridge claimed that a 'national church' was an essential element in the 'constitution of the nation'. This institution was charged with ensuring that all sections of the population were provided with the means of developing moral and intellectual faculties that would illuminate and fortify their practical commitment to the moral values that underpinned the state. Although the national church in England was closely associated with the Church of England, established by law as one pillar of the Tory Anglican 'church state', Coleridge's conception of the 'national church' was more extensive than this. It embraced an educated and educational elite, which included members of the learned professions who were graduates of the universities, as well as the clergy of the Church of England. Coleridge's national church was the institutional form of what he called the 'clerisy', 'an accredited, learned and philosophic *class*' dedicated to nurturing 'a learned and philosophic public' which understood the ends of the state and was committed to performing the duties necessary to advance them. He insisted that while commerce may advance 'civilization', only the ongoing influence of the clerisy would ensure that this is grounded in '*cultivation*', in the 'harmonious development of those qualities and faculties that characterise our *humanity*' (42–3).

The national church was an 'estate' of the realm whose independence was ensured by its possession of property. Unlike landed or commercial property, however, the endowments of the national church were dedicated to *national* rather than *personal* purposes. Coleridge underlined this distinction by describing its property as the 'Nationalty', in contrast to the 'Propriety' held by those who controlled the legislative and executive. The 'Nationalty' provided the means through which the national church performed its functions, and since it was under its corporate control, the clerisy had the means of remaining independent of the influence of government, and of permanent and progressive interests embedded in parliament. Coleridge applied the same image of electromagnetic balance to the relationship between the forces making up the constitution of the state and the national church as he had done to that existing between the different forms of propriety. They are 'the two poles of the same magnet; the magnet itself, which is constituted by them, is the CONSTITUTION of the nation.' The 'nationalty' and 'propriety' form 'the two constituent factors, the opposite, but correspondent and reciprocally supporting, counter-weights, of the *commonwealth*, the existence of the one being the condition, and perfecting, of the rightfulness of the other' (31, 35).

Coleridge saw the national church as a necessary feature of a well-ordered political community and had criticized the French constitution of 1799 for creating a state-funded clergy that would be entirely dependent on government: 'The Church of France is a *standing* church, as its army is a *standing* army.'[8] He argued, however, that the clerisy had a particularly critical role to play in contemporary Britain because the landed classes' capacity to serve as a counterpoise to the commercial interest had been undermined by its positive response to the morally spurious appeals of the spirit of commerce and its intellectual expression in the putative science of political economy.[9] This dangerous development was indicative of a failure in elite education and the need for it to be re-oriented by the true principles of philosophy grounded in religion so it would provide a 'counter-charm to the sorcery of wealth'.[10]

Church and State was published as an unabashedly retrospective contribution to the debate over 'catholic emancipation'. This debate, which erupted from time to time in early-nineteenth-century British politics, reached a crescendo in the late 1820s, and was concluded by the Catholic Emancipation Act of 1829. The term 'catholic emancipation' referred to the repeal of legislation that prevented Roman Catholics from sitting in the British parliament, holding commissions in the armed services and occupying a range of significant civil and juridical offices. Coleridge's ideas about property and political power and the distinction between 'propriety' and 'nationalty' played key roles in his response to catholic emancipation. One the one hand, he believed that it was unjust to deprive Roman Catholic property holders of their electoral rights or to exclude them from military and state offices. This position was an essentially progressive one that rejected conservative claims about the fatal impact of catholic emancipation on the traditional 'constitution in church and state'. On the other hand, Coleridge was adamant that measures to remove penalties imposed on individual catholics should be accompanied by legislative 'securities' which prevented the catholic clergy having access to the nationalty. Since members of the priesthood had taken a vow of celibacy which deprived them of a biological links with the community, and owed allegiance to a foreign sovereign (the Pope), they were effectively removed from membership of the nation and should have no claim on the resources set aside for national purposes. Significantly, however, this prohibition was constitutional rather than theological. That is, the Anglican Church of England's claims to the 'nationalty' rested on its status as a national church, not on the purity of the doctrine it espoused.[11]

Coleridge's commitment to the place of proprietorial interests in legislation and government, his endorsement of the traditional British constitution embracing the Crown, lords and commons, and the privileged position ascribed to the Church of England, all pointed to a conception of politics that had clear affinities with contemporary Toryism and the more diffuse tradition of British conservatism. The way these themes were handled, however, was characteristically complex and subtle. Coleridge's account of the ends of the commonwealth evoked an image of social and political life that is far more humane, liberal and progressive than statements of conservativism that are premised on fundamental inequality and fatally flawed human rationality. Moreover, he saw the interests of permanence and progression as coexisting in ways that potentially advanced both the material and moral ends of the state and did not confine viable change to slow accretions on traditional structures. Coleridge insisted, however, that this potential would only be unlocked if social and political elites received an education that enabled them to see their proprietorial interests in the context of state's role in promoting the material welfare and moral development of all members of the community. Under prevailing conditions, this line of argument entailed an overt critique of both the upper classes and those responsible for their ongoing education. Coleridge referred to socially irresponsible members of the upper classes as 'Jacobinism's quality cousins', likening elites' attitudes to those of radical agitators, but driven in their case by the 'abstract reason' of political economy and the 'bestial passions' of personal self-indulgence.[12] His criticism of the upper classes extended to include the clerisy. While enjoying access to the 'nationalty' it had neglected its educational duty and failed to act as an independent check on backsliding members of the aristocracy and gentry. In other words, the clerisy had become an accomplice of a self-serving elite rather than its intellectual and moral conscience and mentor.[13]

Coleridge's theory of church and state was taken up by reform-minded Liberal Anglicans rather than by traditional Tories, who could not accept his insistence on the national rather than the denominational characteristics of the English Church, or by emerging conservative politicians and writers who could not endorse his strongly critical views of political economy. John Stuart Mill was a sharp critic of Coleridge's economic ideas but his prediction that if Coleridge's 'principles' were to be adopted by the Tories, 'we should not wait long for further reform, even in our organic institutions', suggests that the conservative moment presented in *Church and State* was a critical, liberal, optimistic and progressive one.[14]

CHAPTER EIGHT

Leo Strauss: Theoretical radical, practical liberal–conservative

David Lewis Schaefer

*[C]onservatives look with greater sympathy than liberals on the
particular or particularist and the heterogeneous . . . Inasmuch
as the universalism in politics is founded on the universalism
proceeding from reason, conservatism is frequently characterized
by distrust of reason or by trust in tradition, which as such is
necessarily . . . particular. Conservatism is therefore exposed
to criticism that is guided by the notion of the unity of truth.
Liberals, on the other hand, especially those who know that
their aspirations have their roots in the Western tradition, are not
sufficiently concerned with the fact that that tradition is ever more
being eroded by the very changes in the direction of One World
which they demand or applaud . . .
[L]iberals frequently call themselves progressives. Progressivism
is indeed a better term than liberalism for the opposite to
conservatism. For if conservatism is . . . aversion to change
or distrust of change, its opposite should be identified with
the opposite posture toward change, and not with something
substantive like liberty or liberality.*

The difficulty of defining the difference between liberalism and conservatism ... is particularly great in the United States, since this country came into being through a revolution ... The opposition between conservatism and liberalism had a clear meaning at the time [in Europe] ... [T]he conservatives stood for 'throne and altar', and the liberals stood for popular sovereignty and the strictly nonpublic (private) character of religion. Yet conservatism in this sense is no longer politically important. The conservatism of our age is identical with what originally was liberalism, more or less modified by changes in the direction of present-day liberalism ... Much of what goes now by the name of conservatism has in the last analysis a common root with present-day liberalism and even with Communism. That this is the case would appear most clearly if one were to go back to the origin of modernity, to the break with the premodern tradition that took place in the seventeenth century, or to the quarrel between the ancients and the moderns.[1]

I

Leo Strauss (1899–1973) was arguably the greatest philosophic thinker of the twentieth century. After receiving a doctorate at the University of Hamburg, he worked at an institute devoted to the study of Jewish thought before leaving Germany for England in 1932 and then for America, where he taught at the New School for Social Research and subsequently (for two decades) in the political science department at the University of Chicago. Strauss's most fundamental insight, arrived at in the 1930s, was his rediscovery of the practice of esoteric writing – that is, the strategy of philosophic writers (including the greatest poets) living in preliberal times of concealing their deepest and most challenging thoughts from superficial readers, for purposes of self-protection, pedagogy and respecting the moral and religious foundations of the societies they inhabited.[2] The rediscovery of esotericism in turn enabled Strauss to refute the historicist assumption that every thinker is inevitably the prisoner of the dominant presuppositions of his time and place, so that contemporary readers can learn little about the most important issues from even the greatest thinkers of the past. Instead, when wise men appear to take for granted the dominant assumptions or prejudices of their time (e.g., Aristotle's seeming defense of the naturalness of slavery, or Locke's weakly argued attempt to ground his revolutionary natural-rights doctrine in traditional Christian natural law), a close study of their texts may reveal that this was only window dressing, concealing a continuing, rationally based dialogue about the most fundamental (political, moral and religious) questions in which contemporary readers, whatever their own cultural backgrounds, may still participate. In sum, through his analyses of a wide range of authors – ancient (Plato/Xenophon/Aristophanes/ Thucydides/Aristotle), medieval (notably Maimonides and Alfarabi) and modern (from Machiavelli, Hobbes, Spinoza and Rousseau to Nietzsche and Heidegger) – Strauss restored the study of political philosophy as a living enterprise, rather than a merely antiquarian one.

Ironically, however, in view of the revolutionary character of his discoveries, Strauss has been widely depicted as a conservative, both by some sympathetic friends and (in far greater number, given the political predilections of most Western, and especially Anglo-American, academics over the past century) hostile critics. This impression has been deepened by the fact that in recent decades, several prominent individuals influenced by Strauss's teachings have become prominent in the 'neoconservative' movement.[3]

In this essay I explain why it is inappropriate to label Strauss as a conservative, except in a limited sense – one not incompatible with his having been just as much a liberal, in (what he understood as) the proper sense of that term. Above all, the label misrepresents Strauss as a political partisan, rather than a lover and seeker of wisdom – that is, a philosopher. Although intended to inform a deeper understanding of current political and moral issues, Strauss's writings do not offer a political doctrine. Moreover, since a guiding theme of Strauss's inquiries was the problematic character of modern political philosophy as a whole, in comparison with the thought of the classical political philosophers, he regarded the very dichotomy between liberalism and conservatism, whatever its practical significance, as symptomatic of an unfortunate narrowing of the contemporary intellectual horizon.

II

The above excerpt is taken from Strauss's most extended (albeit brief) treatment of the relation between contemporary liberalism and conservatism in the preface to his 1968 collection of essays *Liberalism Ancient and Modern* (abbreviated as *LAM* here).

The first thing to be noted about this quotation is Strauss's observation that partisans of *both* liberalism and conservatism misunderstand the foundations of their doctrines – wrongly viewing them as theoretically fundamental alternatives, whereas the entire liberal–conservative dichotomy arose out of the eighteenth-century Enlightenment (more precisely, as the legacy of the French Revolution). Viewed in light of the history of the Great

Tradition of Western thought (encompassing the legacies of both Athens and Jerusalem), what self-styled liberals and conservatives have in common at the theoretical level (and even, Strauss suggests, with liberal democracy's greatest post-war antagonist, communism) outweighs what divides them.

The second thing to note is that Strauss nowhere identifies himself with either side of the liberal–conservative divide. Indeed, after noting the limitations of each outlook, he suggests that the very title 'conservatism' suffers by comparison with 'liberalism', since the former (like 'progressivism') signifies a mere contentless attitude, while the latter denotes a 'substantive', generally admired good, 'liberty or liberality', which he adds 'is still used in its premodern sense, especially in the expression "liberal education"'. (Strauss devotes the first two essays in *LAM* to the theme of liberal education.)

Finally, it should be remarked that to the extent the quotation signifies anything of Strauss's own inclination, in view of his lifelong devotion to the pursuit of truth by reliance on unaided reason, it indicates a closer affinity to liberalism than to conservatism, given the liability of the latter to the charge that its attachment to tradition is purchased at the expense of the distrust of reason – and hence (it would appear) of an opposition to philosophy itself. (In his 1947 essay 'On the Intention of Rousseau',[4] Strauss articulates Rousseau's attempt to balance the claims of rationalism and traditionalism in his *First Discourse* (1750) by restoring the classical understanding of the need for philosophers to restrict the *public* expression of their discoveries.)

III

How, then, did Strauss become known as a conservative? How did his writings particularly attract readers of a conservative orientation, or even move some of them towards what is now regarded as a conservative position?

In the third chapter of his most popularly accessible book, *Natural Right and History* (hereafter *NRH*),[5] Strauss emphasizes that philosophy, and hence the pursuit of a natural standard of right or justice, could arise only as a consequence of the *doubt* of all established authority: 'The first things and the right way cannot become questionable or the object of a quest, or philosophy cannot emerge, or nature cannot be discovered, if authority as such is not doubted' (84). Unlike their modern, revolutionary counterparts, Strauss observes, '[t]he classical philosophers did full justice to the great truth underlying the identification of the good with the ancestral,' as instanced by the case of Socrates, who 'was a very conservative man as far as the ultimate practical conclusions of his political philosophy were concerned'.[6] Yet, he adds, the comic playwright Aristophanes 'pointed to the truth [in *The Clouds*] by suggesting that Socrates' fundamental premise [i.e., taking one's bearings by nature rather than customary authority] could induce a son to beat up his own father' (93). In other words, recognizing the incapacity of most human beings to guide themselves properly by reliance on reason rather than tradition, the classical philosophers made a radical distinction between the *intellectual* freedom that philosophy requires and the *practical* subjection to law, and outward respect for customary moral and religious beliefs, that are the precondition of civilized life.

It is in this connection that Strauss's rediscovery of esoteric writing, and his emphasis on the distinction between classical and modern political philosophy, achieves its greatest significance. Ever since the loss of awareness of that form of writing, beginning at the end of the eighteenth century, philosophical 'scholars', along with most readers, had underestimated the radical character of the *thought* of the classical philosophers, recognition of which is essential to appreciating its transhistorical importance (and hence its potential significance for our own lives). In contrast with their ancient counterparts, the modern philosophers whose thought generated the Enlightenment, beginning in the sixteenth century with Machiavelli and Montaigne, envisioned a much more active role for philosophy in transforming or 'rationalizing' popular political, moral and religious beliefs – culminating ultimately, it was hoped, in something like the modern liberal regime (exemplified, at its peak, by the American Constitution), in which the very need for concealment of the truth discovered by reason would have disappeared.

Unfortunately, despite its manifest success in elevating the political and economic lot of ordinary people, as well as providing unparalleled legal freedom of thought and discourse, in much of the Western and 'Westernized' world (including parts of Asia), the liberal project fell short of fulfilling its originators' hopes of 'solving' the human problem. Instead, owing to certain deficiencies in the project itself, that project was modified by what Strauss termed two subsequent 'waves' of modernity, the latter of which culminated in the intellectual crisis that Strauss identifies in the opening pages of *NRH* – the denial of the capacity of reason to provide meaningful standards, grounded in nature, for distinguishing the just and unjust.[7] Theoretically, the deepest expositor of this crisis, as Strauss portrays it, is Nietzsche.[8] Nietzsche both identified and radicalized the problem inherent in the liberal project that underlay the historicist rejection of natural right to which Strauss directs our attention in the introduction and opening chapter of *NRH*. In twentieth-century America, that rejection culminated in the thoughtless liberal relativism (even more widespread in our own era) that groundlessly assumes, Strauss points out, that if all so-called 'values' are seen as equally valid (or invalid), then we are obliged to tolerate all moral opinions and 'civilizations' as equally meritorious (rather than impose our views on others) (*NRH* 5–6). In reality, liberal relativism would entail that tolerance has no deeper justification than intolerance. But the original root of the contemporary rejection of natural right was not mere liberal naiveté. Rather, for Strauss, it grew out of a certain *moral* attitude that he articulated in a 1941 lecture, unpublished during his lifetime, on 'German Nihilism'.[9]

As Strauss explained in this lecture, despite the unspeakable evils in which German nihilism culminated in the form of Nazism – just as Rousseau's thought had had the unforeseen effect of generating the horrors of the French Revolution – it originated in a revulsion, among idealistic youth, at the seeming lowness of the aims of modern, Western (English and French) 'civilization': mere comfort and security. In contrast to the liberal goal of an 'open society' in which national differences (and hence the possibility of war) withered away, the partisans of German nihilism believed 'that the root of all moral life is essentially ... the *closed* society' which called for the utmost sacrifices from its members – above all, in war (358 [emphasis added]).

Strauss, needless to say, had nothing but abhorrence for Nazism, just as he despised Communist totalitarianism. But he denied that Western, liberal principles could be defended against the threat of nihilism simply by repeating eighteenth-century formulas like 'the greatest happiness of the greatest number' or even 'the rights of man.' Instead, he maintained that our very determination to preserve what is best in modern constitutional democracy requires a rethinking of the grounds of that regime – and an endeavor to consider how it might be *enriched* by reconsideration of the original foundations of natural right in the writings of the classical philosophers.

Of Strauss's own devotion to the preservation of constitutional democracy there can be no reasonable doubt. In response to the Hegelian–Marxist thinker Alexandre Kojève's exaltation of the universal, homogeneous state, Strauss remarked that 'liberal or constitutional democracy comes closer to what the classics demanded than any alternative that is viable in our age'.[10] In a lecture on 'The Three Waves of Modernity', he observed that even though Nietzsche's powerful 'critique of modern rationalism', out of which 'the theory of liberal democracy as well as of communism' had 'originated ... cannot be dismissed or forgotten ... liberal democracy, in contradistinction to communism and fascism, derives powerful support from ... the premodern thought of our western tradition'.[11] Nonetheless, the discovery of 'a solid basis for liberalism', properly understood, which Strauss represented as his aim, would require what he termed 'a very great effort'.[12]

As we have seen, Strauss never identified himself as a partisan of conservatism as *opposed* to liberalism. Nonetheless, in the context of the twentieth-century Anglo-American academy, Strauss's challenge to relativism held great appeal to those who aimed to 'conserve' the Western philosophic, religious, and political traditions (whatever the differences among and within those traditions, which he aimed to illuminate rather than deny). Additionally, as regards specific matters of public policy, as distinguished from fundamental intellectual principles, Strauss typically leaned towards the conservative side of American politics, even though he wrote nothing about domestic issues.[13] And while not all of his students or those otherwise influenced by him were conservative, those who were liberals, in present-day parlance, were *moderate* liberals, just as conservatives who understood his thought eschewed extremism (and the notion of a 'Straussian Marxist' would be an oxymoron). The chief reason for Strauss's apparently nonliberal tendency, I suggest, lies in the reinterpretation of liberalism during the past century to mean 'progressivism' – reflecting the dogmatic, potentially illiberal denial that there are any fixed limits to the proper scope of government, to the advancement of equality, to the elimination of human conflict or to the perfectibility of human nature.[14] Despite the fundamental differences that Strauss articulated among the classical and medieval political philosophers and the three waves of modern thinkers who succeeded them, it is unlikely that even those who harbored the grandest hopes for human improvement would have subscribed to such naive and dangerously misleading beliefs. In other words, they were not utopians (Marx and Engels are the obvious exceptions – but in view of Marx's acknowledgement that his goal was not to 'interpret' the world but 'to *change* it',[15] neither of them can properly be described as philosophers, as distinguished from ideologues).

While devoting himself to the study of classic texts, Strauss was by no means oblivious to the practical problems of statesmanship in his own time, nor sparing of admiration for its greatest practitioners, such as Churchill. Having articulated the deficiencies of modern liberalism even in its original form (e.g., in his treatment of Locke in *NRH*, chapter 5), Strauss applauded not only its conduciveness to justice towards individuals, but also the opportunity it provided for cultivating the life of the mind. Strauss also called for a return to a genuinely empirical, 'Aristotelian' mode of political study that 'views political things in the perspective of the citizen' rather than the ostensibly neutral theorist.[16] Inspired by this approach, numerous scholars have undertaken careful, often profound, inquiries into American political thought, constitutional law, and political practice, as well as international relations.

Without in any way encouraging 'an unmanly contempt for politics' (*LAM* 22), and hence for partisan activity, Strauss taught all those who were open to learning to see beyond the liberal–conservative dichotomy. Like Socrates, he combined radicalism in thought with a teaching of moderation in practice. Since 'wisdom cannot be separated from moderation,' he observed, it requires 'unhesitating loyalty to a decent constitution and … the cause of constitutionalism,' even as it liberates us from 'visionary' political expectations (*LAM* 24). In seeking to enhance the cause of liberal constitutionalism, and at the same time to preserve a serious appreciation and understanding of the philosophic life, Strauss was both a liberal and a conservative in the truest sense.

CHAPTER NINE

Michael Oakeshott
'On Being Conservative'

Ephraim Podoksik

The self-government of men of passionate belief and enterprise is apt to break down when it is most needed. It often suffices to resolve minor collisions of interest, but beyond these it is not to be relied upon. A more precise and a less easily corrupted ritual is required to resolve the massive collisions which our manner of living is apt to generate and to release us from the massive frustrations in which we are apt to become locked. The custodian of this ritual is 'the government', and the rules it imposes are 'the law'. One may imagine a government engaged in the activity of an arbiter in cases of collisions of interest but doing its business without the aid of laws, just as one may imagine a game without rules and an umpire who was appealed to in cases of dispute and who on each occasion merely used his judgment to devise ad hoc a way of releasing the disputants from their mutual frustration. But the diseconomy of such an arrangement is so obvious that it could only be expected to occur to those inclined to believe the ruler to be supernaturally inspired and to those disposed to attribute to him a quite different voice – that of leader, or tutor, or manager. At all events the disposition to be conservative

in respect of government is rooted in the belief that where
government rests upon the acceptance of the current activities
and beliefs of its subjects, the only appropriate manner of ruling is
by making and enforcing rules of conduct . . .
To govern, then, as the conservative understands it, is to provide
a vinculum juris *for those manners of conduct which, in the*
circumstances, are least likely to result in a frustrating collision
of interests; to provide redress and means of compensation for
those who suffer from others behaving in a contrary manner;
sometimes to provide punishment for those who pursue their
own interests regardless of the rules; and, of course, to provide a
sufficient force to maintain the authority of an arbiter of this kind.
Thus, governing is recognized as a specific and limited activity; not
the management of an enterprise, but the rule of those engaged
in a great diversity of self-chosen enterprises. It is not concerned
with concrete persons, but with activities; and with activities only
in respect of their propensity to collide with one another. It is
not concerned with moral right and wrong, it is not designed to
make men good or even better; it is not indispensable on account
of 'the natural depravity of mankind' but merely because of their
current disposition to be extravagant; its business is to keep its
subjects at peace with one another in the activities in which they
have chosen to seek their happiness.[1]

I

Michael Oakeshott (1901–1990) was a prominent twentieth-century British philosopher who wrote on diverse topics, such as philosophy of history, philosophy of science, aesthetics and ethics. He initially followed the footsteps of the tradition of British Absolute Idealism in the vein of F. H. Bradley and Bernard Bosanquet, but later developed a significantly more sceptical outlook, influenced, among other trends, by German neo-Kantianism and the Anglophone philosophy of language. In his philosophy, he diagnosed the modern condition as that of radical plurality characterized by the coexistence of autonomous and mutually irrelevant views of the world: modes of experience.

However, he acquired prominence among a broader audience first as a political thinker. Political philosophy was indeed one of his major preoccupations. For several decades, he taught the history of political thought, first as a lecturer in the History Faculty of the University of Cambridge, and then as a professor of political science at the London School of Economics. Regarded as one of the finest Hobbes interpreters, in 1946, he edited Hobbes's *Leviathan* for Blackwell. And his own essays, collected in the 1962 volume *Rationalism in Politics and Other Essays*, earned him the reputation of a paradigmatic conservative thinker.

Yet Oakeshott turned out to be a very enigmatic conservative. As he outlined the postulates of his political philosophy in the treatise *On Human Conduct* (1975), many commentators began to doubt whether he could be called a conservative at all. A respectable school of interpretation has come to regard him as a liberal.

To reconcile between these two conflicting perceptions, one could indeed argue that Oakeshott's attitude evolved: an (illiberal) conservative in the beginning, he later turned into a (conservative) liberal. The difference between the two positions can be described as follows. Illiberal conservatism conceives itself as an alternative to liberalism. It is inegalitarian rather than egalitarian, and corporatist rather than individualist. On the level of policy it is sympathetic to limited monarchy and influential aristocracy; it defends the established church, advocates power politics in foreign affairs, and generally favours protectionist economic arrangements. 'Conservative liberalism', by contrast, signifies an anti-progressivist current within liberalism broadly conceived. It accepts the core liberal arrangements such as civil liberties, equality before law and free enterprise. But it combines those with gradualism and the respect for tradition and religious belief. For a conservative liberal, any radical pursuit of liberal slogans is detrimental to liberal arrangements themselves.

Now, whereas it is true that the development of Oakeshott's ideas was on the whole in the direction of a more liberal world view, I believe that this story requires certain modification. Actually, conservative as well as liberal elements can be found in both Oakeshott's earlier and later writings. The difference between the earlier and later Oakeshott lies, in my view, not in the presence or absence of either conservative or liberal dispositions, but in the manner in which the two interact. While in Oakeshott's earlier writings they coexist as two disparate lines, in later ones this original dissonance is transformed into a more or less harmonious whole, in which the melody is played by conservative liberalism while the residues of the illiberal conservative attitude act as an occasional counterpoint.

II

In his introduction to a 1939 anthology of contemporary political doctrines, Oakeshott argued that there existed a fundamental gap between two types of doctrines. On the one hand, there were those 'which hand over to the arbitrary will of a society's self-appointed leaders the planning of its entire life'.[2] Communism, Fascism and National Socialism belonged to that category. There is no doubt that Oakeshott was repelled by these doctrines, giving preference to the more decent ones: 'those which not only refuse to hand over the destiny of a society to any set of officials but also consider the whole notion of planning the destiny of a society to be both stupid and immoral'.[3] One such doctrine was 'Representative Democracy'. Yet it was not the only possible alternative to totalitarianism. There was in fact another option: 'Catholicism'. The political embodiments of this doctrine were, in Oakeshott's view, Ireland, Portugal and pre-*Anschluss* Austria.

Although both Representative Democracy and Catholicism profess profound antipathy towards the totalitarian sentiment, the differences between the two are significant. According to Oakeshott, Catholicism is related 'to the historic doctrine of Conservatism'.[4] Representative Democracy, by contrast, is related to liberalism, even if its liberalism should not be confused with 'merely the history of the rise and dominance of a peculiar narrow brand of individualism', and even if a certain so-to-speak conservative aspect is embedded in it, for 'it has the advantage of all the others in that it has shown itself capable of changing without perishing in the process, and it has the advantage (denied to all others save Catholicism) of not being the hasty product of a generation but of belonging to a long and impressive tradition of thought'.[5]

Two more differences can be uncovered from Oakeshott's depiction. The first is cultural-geographical. Catholicism is a political doctrine widespread in continental Europe. Representative Democracy, by contrast, if one judges from the list of thinkers chosen by Oakeshott to exemplify it, such as Paine, Mill, Lincoln, Cobbett, Green and Tocqueville, belongs more properly to the Anglo-American sphere. The second difference is their relative strengths and weaknesses. In Catholicism, Oakeshott emphasizes intellectual coherence (noting however that this doctrine may be outdated[6]); by contrast, he denies any philosophical value to the doctrine of representative democracy, yet praises the latter's practical vitality.

These two doctrines appear to reflect what I call illiberal conservatism and conservative liberalism. The earlier Oakeshott had good words to say about each of them. Both were for him legitimate and interesting self-expressions of the Western civilization. But if as an Englishman he appeared to sympathize with the moral benefits of the long tradition of Anglo-American liberalism, as a philosopher he seemed to be more attracted to the authoritarian conservatism of European lineage, for he consistently regarded the European continental philosophical tradition as superior to what Britain or America were able to offer.

The polemical essays that Oakeshott published in the late 1940s and early 1950s can be assigned either to one or the other of these disparate doctrines. On the one hand, there are essays dedicated to the critique of rationalism: 'Rationalism in Politics', 'The Tower of Babel', 'Rational

Conduct' and 'Political Education'. Their common motif is a harsh criticism of modern civilization for its preference of reflective engineering over pre-reflective spontaneity, of technique over tradition. These essays can claim illiberal conservative lineage because of the following features.

First, Oakeshott's criticism appears to be directed not against specific features of modern civilization but against its overall tendency towards rationalism. Second, he does not draw a distinction between liberal and anti-liberal tendencies of modernity. The notion of human rights is ridiculed by him no less than that of equality or racial purity; the inexperienced rulers of modern times seem to be regarded by him as inferior in quality to the experienced aristocracies of the past; and even Friedrich Hayek is suspected of being too much of a rationalist. Third, he allows occasional remarks which may point to a degree of social conservatism. Thus, he regrets the demise of parental authority.[7] The intellectual sources of this conservative pessimism can be found in various stands of European continental anti-liberalism, and especially in life philosophy.[8]

This attitude can be contrasted with the one expressed in the essay 'The Political Economy of Freedom' which pays homage to the ideas of the free-market Chicago economist Henry C. Simons. In it, Oakeshott discusses the specifically English idea of freedom and the economic policy which would properly fit it. The heart of English freedom is for him the dispersal of power in a society ensured by the general acceptance of the rule of law. In the area of economics, the maintenance of this freedom requires protecting private property, curbing the power of monopolies (especially trade unions) and reining in inflation. Occasionally he inserts a Burkean-like traditionalism. Thus, one of the forms of the diffusion of power in a society is said to be 'a diffusion of authority between past, present and future'.[9] But the term 'conservatism' is absent from the essay. Simons, Oakeshott tells us, called himself a liberal and democrat, the follower of Adam Smith, Bentham, Mill, Sidgwick, Tocqueville, Burckhardt and Acton, even if he 'suffered from neither of the current afflictions of liberalism – ignorance of who its true friends are, and the nervy conscience which extends a senile and indiscriminate welcome to everyone who claims to be on the side of "progress"'.[10] Being averse to the word 'liberal', Oakeshott refers to the view that he himself appears to espouse as that of 'the English libertarian'.[11]

'The Political Economy of Freedom' exemplifies the conservative–liberal aspect of the earlier Oakeshott. Its overall character is different from that of the other essays of the same period included in *Rationalism in Politics*, even if some common ground can be found to reconcile its liberal mood with the pessimistic anti-rationalism of the others. It also appears that in this period the liberal mood was not dominant in Oakeshott. The fact that the essay was included in *Rationalism in Politics* should not mislead: that volume appeared in 1962, after Oakeshott had adopted a more positive stance towards liberalism and modern society. In the early 1950s, however, he was less sure. In another and less libertarian essay of that period, he could argue, for example, that 'there is little evidence that competition itself produces diversity – rather the reverse'.[12]

III

Yet towards the mid-1950s, Oakeshott's approach changes significantly. First, conservative liberalism and illiberal conservatism swap roles, with the former acquiring pre-eminence. Moreover, Oakeshott clearly attempts to clear the path for a more coherent outlook so that illiberal elements could be integrated within the overall liberal world view.

The essay 'On Being Conservative' (1956) is the key indicator of this change. It presents an idea of government which can clearly be identified as belonging to conservative liberalism. Yet this liberalism is taken to be the only realistic form of political *conservatism*. According to Oakeshott, the conservative disposition in general is the disposition to enjoy the present for its own sake and on account of our mere familiarity with it. When applied to the sphere of politics, this disposition does not need to find expression in what were usually perceived as ideological corner stones of conservative politics, for example, an organic theory of human society, a belief in the sinfulness of human nature, royalism or Anglicanism.[13]

Just twenty years earlier, Oakeshott would see most of these features as congenial to the political doctrine of 'Catholicism'. Now all of this is declared inessential. To be a conservative in politics now does not mean pursuing this or that political ideal, but merely maintaining the conditions under which citizens are free to conduct their present activities with a minimal degree of disruption. As he argued, governing 'is not concerned with moral right and wrong, it is not designed to make men good or even better … its business is to keep its subjects at peace with one another in the activities in which they have chosen to seek their happiness'.[14]

In principle, specific contents of 'conservative' politics can differ from one historical context to another. But Oakeshott is interested in what it may mean in the context of modernity, which he conceives as a condition where citizens endowed with highly developed individuality are bent on pursuing choices of their own. The modern situation is characterized by great diversity of preferences. In such a situation, the proper role of government is to prevent collisions between the activities of the citizens without imposing on them a single correct way of life.

Moreover, this vision of government is not presented as an unavoidable concession to a problematic condition. For the diversity of individual preferences is not merely diagnosed by Oakeshott; it is also praised. Earlier he described modernity as contaminated by rationalism, but now it is justified through individualism. In the essay 'The Masses in Representative Democracy' (1957), written about the same time as 'On Being Conservative', Oakeshott no longer contrasts the problematic rationalistic present with a somewhat distant non-rationalistic past.[15] Rather, modernity itself is torn between two contrary moral visions: the morality of individuality and the morality of anti-individuality. Oakeshott stands for the former and believes that it has every chance to prevail.

Thus, towards the mid-1950s, Oakeshott established the basic parameters of his mature political outlook. Twenty years later, in *On Human Conduct*, he developed on their basis a full-fledged political theory. The heart of this theory is the distinction between two kinds of association: enterprise association and civil association. The key difference between the two is their raison d'être: for the enterprise association it is pursuit of a common purpose; for the civil association it is subscription to common rules. The enterprise association usually has rules too. But these rules are supposed to be instrumental in reaching the association's purpose; they will be amended if they do not serve that purpose. In the civil association, by contrast, the rules are non-instrumental, for there is no purpose to achieve.

The modern state includes within it a great variety of associations, most of which are likely to be enterprise associations of different kinds. Yet the state itself should not take this character. The reason is that the state is a comprehensive compulsory association. Considering it as an enterprise association, that is, assigning to it a specific purpose, would be incompatible with the principal circumstance of modern life: the great diversity of individual characters each prone to explore their own individuality in a self-chosen way. Whatever the state's declared purpose, some members of the state will dissent from it and as a consequence feel that they are forced to subscribe to a project in which they are unwilling to take part. This would violate their integrity.

Indeed, not every modern person possesses strong individuality. Some persons lacking in individuality are more than happy to be told what purpose to pursue. Many features of the modern state reflect the existence of such people. However, the principal protagonist of modernity is 'the individual' who desires to pursue freely chosen purposes and projects. For such a person the forced membership in the state can be acceptable only if it is considered as a civil association, that is, association in terms of non-instrumental rules of conduct rather than in terms of purposes.

The theory of civil association has been generally interpreted as a liberal theory of the state. Such an interpretation is not unavoidable. It is possible to insert in the civil association a more conservative content. Two aspects of the theory may lead us in this direction. First, while members of the civil association are expected to 'assent' to the authority of the rulers, they do not necessarily choose them, and the rulers are not necessarily accountable to the ruled. The theory is therefore indifferent to the form of government: it can be democratic or authoritarian. Second, whereas the rules of the association cannot be changed in view of serving some purpose, they can be amended in order to reflect changes in current practices of the society. It is indeed possible to imagine that despite the diversity of enterprises, certain practices would be considered as widespread enough to be established as legal norms. This may lead to a 'social conservative' persecution of 'deviant' practices.

These are however relatively marginal possibilities. The rhetoric and logic of the theory rather follow the tradition of Cold War liberalism with its dichotomy of liberalism and totalitarianism. The distinction between the two kinds of association is especially reminiscent of Hayek's distinction between telocracies and nomocracies. The emphasis on the importance of freedom and individuality is the dominant aspect of Oakeshott's theory outlined in *On Human Conduct*.

If one looks for a connection between this and Oakeshott's earlier illiberal conservatism, one should rather consider his rejection of purpose. The value of purposelessness was a consistent motif of his thinking in all areas. In the context of politics, the idea of purposelessness played out in two different ways in the earlier and later Oakeshott. In the first half of the twentieth century, the emphasis on purposelessness tended to indicate anti-totalitarian illiberal conservatism. This conservatism rejected liberal as well as totalitarian ideologies because it assigned to both one common feature: the rationalistic pursuit of a social ideal. Oakeshott's initial uneasiness regarding liberalism was to a great degree the result of the latter's preoccupation with 'progress'. Conservatism, by contrast, emphasized the sinfulness of human nature and the fundamental imperfection of human societies.

In the second half of the twentieth century, however, many currents in liberalism adopted a more pessimistic and anti-progressivist line. The belief in progress ceased to be the crucial test for possessing the liberal mind. As a consequence, it became possible to integrate purposelessness within a liberal political world view. Oakeshott's *On Human Conduct* can be counted among the most interesting examples of such integration.

PART THREE

Conservatism in contexts

CHAPTER TEN

Reflections on cross-currents of Russian conservatism

Elena Chebankova

Every nation, just like every individual, has its own inner strength and can survive by it in a wider world; yet one needs to act in order to be alive. And to do that one needs to be in full command with his body parts. Say this to those who blindly admire the customs of other peoples [Europeans]. Tell them that we too can live like the rest [of Europe], if we free ourselves from the alien/ foreign theories that constrain our life and adopt just one founding principle – free competition of agents – and ensure that law and order protects all activity and allows free development. They will object and cite Proudhon and Lois-Blanc ... They will refer to the rudeness and ignorance of our people, as though other countries that boast progressive development have fully educated masses ... No, the problem is not the one of education. English squires of the past century were not more educated than contemporary Russian landowners; the trick is in the organisation of socio- political life and in self-reliance of people. Only self-governed life creates real characters; only such life develops civic spirit, true education, and wealth.[1]

In our day enlightened intelligentsia is ruled by generalisations, and seeks a logical constitution to life and society on universal [European] principles. These are the new fetishes that have taken the place of the old idols ... Our modern idols are phrases and generalities, such as Liberty, Equality, and Fraternity, with their variations and extensions ... Faith in abstract [European] principles is the prevailing error of our time. This error consists in the dogmatic and absolute faith by which we disregard the facts of life with all its conditions and needs, ignoring distinctions of time and place, the characteristics of individuals, and the peculiarities of history.[2]

Political and intellectual life in nineteenth-century Russia was preoccupied with Russia's backwardness vis-a-vis Europe in multifarious political, institutional, social, economic, technological and industrial matters. Russia's decisive input into the victory over Napoleon, the 1814 entry of the Russian Tsar Alexander I and his army to Paris and the country's prominent role in the 1815 Vienna Congress solidified Russia's position as the leading European power at the international level. At the same time, it highlighted domestic socio-economic backwardness and turned this problem into a painful political dilemma for the intellectuals. Hence, existential questions such as *Who are we? What is the foundation stone of our past that defines the main parameters of our present and future?* and *How does that past, present, and future relate to the fate of Europe?* became central. The attempts to answer those questions created significant ruptures in Russia's intellectual and political scene.

In this light, the study of Russian conservatism presents the challenge of accounting for its various cross-currents. Examining the problem in very broad terms, we can conditionally split Russian conservatism in two main branches: liberal and statist. Among intellectuals in nineteenth-century Russia, Mikhail Katkov (1818–87), editor of the *Russian Messenger* (*Russkii Vestnik*) journal, could speak for the liberal conservative, or the 'reactionary liberal', branch. Konstantin Pobedonostsev (1827–1907), the over prosecutor of the Holy Synod, is the most eloquent representative of the bureaucratic statist conservative branch. Both philosophical streams have been occupying a legitimate place in the family of conservative thought in Russia since the nineteenth century and together comprise the intellectual tradition of Russian conservatism.

The liberal branch of conservatism often exhibits intellectual intersections with conservative nationalism, pressing for the gradual development of the Russian state and society in the uniquely Russian tradition, as Mikhail

Katkov points out in his opening extract. Nevertheless, it is also clear that this type of conservatism admires the political evolution of the West and views Russia as part of Europe (albeit with some serious restrictions which are outlined in the following). Being on a similar wavelength with nationalism and liberalism, Katkov, like other liberal conservatives, praised individualism and self-reliance, believing that Russia could begin her revival and flourish by improving the status of each individual.

The statist dimension of Russian conservatism also seeks to integrate the various periods of Russia's evolution and establish a path for the future that could most accurately reflect and encapsulate the country's past. Yet it selects values in a different order of priorities. First, it considers a strong and viable state as the epitome of Russian political evolution. Second, it refuses to accept a European legacy for Russia, viewing Russian civilization as a self-sufficient and separate universe. In that light, thinkers of this kind posit that the values of European liberalism are detrimental to Russia's development and progress – a point of view illustrated by the second quotation above. This chapter discusses all of these dimensions of Russian conservatism.

Views towards Western Europe

It becomes clear from the opening extracts that Russian conservatism in general, much like any other form of conservatism, claims that each society's intellectual, cultural and aesthetic life grows organically from a people's tradition and history. Such traditions give societies their unique identity and spirit (*Volkgeist* or *Volkstum,* to deploy the German romantic terminology), and have their own absolute value. Despite this, however, a complex attitude towards Western Europe has been a source of division in nineteenth- and twentieth-century Russian political thought, and for conservatives in particular.

The Western European 'question' concerns not only the realm of international relations and politics but also more significant metaphysical issues of individual psychological character and wider problems of cultural and social anthropology. While liberal conservatism seeks to integrate Russia's tradition with some elements of Western European political development, its contemporary statist and pre-existing reactionary counterpart actively backs away from Europe, emphasizing the particularity of Russian civilization and her unique historic path. This approach also divorces Russian conservatism from the liberals who regard Russia as an essential but 'confused' or 'broken' part of Europe that must mend her developmental trajectory by rejoining the 'right' side of history pursued by the West.

Both Katkov and Pobedonostsev have left an ample intellectual legacy in Russia. A large number of contemporary Russian conservatives who follow Katkov's line argue that Russia represents part of European civilization that could and should develop a dialogue with its European sister stream. However, just as with Katkov, their idea of a dialogue does not involve intellectual, cultural and political submission. They view it as an exchange between equal partners who mutually enrich each other's visions through their ideas and experiences. These thinkers view Russia as part of the broad European civilization which parted ways when Constantinople succeeded Rome in 330 AD and the Christian Church experienced a Great schism in 1054. Nonetheless, the Greek–Roman–Celtic West and the Hellenistic–Byzantine–Slavic Russia remain two parallel, and intricately intertwined, branches of European heritage. Geographically, they share the continent. Intellectually, they sustain 2,000 years of common culture and history that evolved via dialogue, conflict, cooperation and competition.[3]

Common to this line of thought is the idea of Russia saving Western Europe from decline and degradation. Most conservative philosophers of the nineteenth century and beyond ponder the question of moral and ethical foundations that could allow Europe to remain 'European'. They also harbour hopes that Russia is endowed with the ultimate mission of protecting Europe's political and cultural heritage. The latter includes the Christian foundations of morality and a pluralistic approach to the organization of human life, as well as the negative foundations of liberty that stand in stark opposition to positive pressures towards self-actualization pursued by the contemporary politics of identity. Just as during the nineteenth century Russian nationalist conservatives offered salvation to Europe, Russia's contemporary liberal conservatives hope to guard Europe's freedom and individuality from the pressures of globalization and act as an anchor of traditional European morality.

The statist branch of Russia's conservatism, on the other hand, holds a different position. To this day, this thought represents the intellectual legacy of Nikolay Karamzin (1766–1826), who viewed Russia as an 'organic, separate, national entity which was radically different from ... other countries with regard to customs, outlook, laws, and way of life'[4]. Pobedonostsev's vocal scepticism on the universal applicability of Western political patterns, which is clearly articulated in the opening extract, therefore was not original but highly instrumental to the policy and politics of his age. While admiring political forms found, for example, in France and England, Pobedonostsev did not regard these as models to be transferred to Russia. He argued that 'laws and legal institutions should always conform strictly to the national traditions of a given society'.[5] Alexandr Dugin, a contemporary Russian philosopher whose ideas largely inherit the conservatism of Konstantin Pobedonostsev, sustains this line by arguing that Russia must develop her own intellectual path. She must become isolated from the stream of European philosophy, which sustains 'someone else's ontology' and narrates 'someone else's glories and dramas'. Dugin concludes that Russia joined Western philosophical discussions almost at the very close of 'modernity'. Hence, to break the vicious cycle of borrowing, Russia must develop her own epistemology that could provide a conceptual matrix for her distinct ontology.[6]

Civilization and the Russian world

The task of preserving Russian civilization's distinctiveness thus represents the main theme of contemporary and earlier Russian conservatism. All streams of Russian conservatism subscribe to the idea of the *Russian World* that ought to represent a separate self-sufficient civilization. Deliberations on the nature of civilization and its divergence from the idea of the nation follow as a result of this intellectual endeavour. This continues the quest of Russia's early conservatives concerning the nature of Russia's difference from Western Europe. Boris Mezhuev claims that the difference in eschatology separates nations from civilizations. Following Kant and J. S. Mill, he reminds us that nations require some form of civic maturity that signifies the 'passing of traditional society', the end of barbarity and the negation of 'nature' by a 'republican order'. Simultaneously, a nation sees its collective goals in the dialogical transfer of culture, knowledge and ethics as well as in the preservation of its political integrity, thus rebelling against the idea of universal political systems.[7]

The category 'civilization', on the other hand, is starkly distinct from that of 'a nation'. Mezhuev further claims that, while a nation requires some form of civic maturity with its visible apex in the formation of the nation-state, civilization demands the opposite dynamic.[8] Civilization necessitates a *faith* in the unclear but predestined 'End of History' that binds nation-participants in a universal push towards creating a perfect order, peace and happiness. That historic endeavour requires participants to develop a universal logic in the application of political forms and to exercise a common *Kultur*, to use the Fichtean idea, which expresses true common goals of unity. This approach injects a transcendental flavour into the very notion of civilization. In contrast to the rigid rationality of a nation, civilization requires mere *faith* in the natural ability of its participants to accept their chosen universal order based on the goodness of their chosen epistemology. The movement of civilization through time represents the will of history itself, whose true intentions and logic are unknown to the participants.

At this point, Russian conservatism of all varieties denies that Russia could join the Western trajectory at the level of civilizational faith. The main lines of ethical rupture lie in Western postmodernity. Russian conservatism struggles with the contemporary redefinition of traditional human anthropology, the excessive politicization of gender and sexuality and the prevalence of anti-Christian cultural and political tendencies. Russian conservatism is sceptical and critical about the acceleration of Western politics of identity that, while attending to the problems of subaltern minorities, generates a substantial group of the 'silent majority'. The latter is reluctant to redefine the norms of tradition but remains silent due to the stifling atmosphere of 'political correctness' that almost excludes a traditionalist viewpoint from the newly formed political consensus.

Anthropocentrism

It could be argued that, much like its Western counterpart, Russian philosophy is highly anthropocentric. Our opening extracts suggest that deliberations on the relationship between the individual and society and between the individual and national character compose another key aspect of Russian conservatism. Starting with the Slavophile thinkers, Russia's most prominent philosophers, such as Fyodor Dostoevsky, Leo Tolstoy, Nicolay Berdyaev, Leo Shestov, G. Florovsky, Peter Florensky, placed man at the centre of their reflections.

However, the two strands of conservatism were distinct in their anthropocentrism. Katkov's opening statement suggests that he was a 'convinced individualist for whom social progress depended entirely on the energy and creative ability of men'.[9] Following this trend, the subsequent liberal conservatism of the twentieth century also accentuated individualism and individual rights.[10] Representatives of the liberal conservative intellectual branch – Nicolas Berdyaev, Semyon Frank, Sergei Bulgakov, Alexander Izgoev – believed that Russia's future lies in the spiritual revival of its people and the resurrection of core traditions of compassionate humanism. Theirs was a middle way between radical liberals of the age and the reactive isolationism of statist conservatives. Curiously, the contemporary Russian Orthodox Church also sustains this view. Russian patriarch Cyril insists in most of his speeches that individual revival, constant work on improving one's soul and conscientious attempts at perfecting the individual's environment are the building blocks of Russia's revival and survival as a state and civilization. It is through individual effort that the community could thrive and develop.

At the same time, while speaking about the values of individualism, we must make an important qualification in recognition of the particular Russian understanding of this term. The focus on the individual was of a particular type. Liberal conservatives, such as Berdyaev, redefine the rationalistic anthropology of the Western individual by emphasizing the ideas of compassion, suffering and love as definitive features of a human soul. Hence, the Cartesian *cogito ergo sum* that defined Western individual rationality during the period of modernity is replaced in Berdyaev with *senito ergo sum* (I feel therefore I am) as a definitive and desirable feature of Russian individualism.[11] Liberal conservatives ponder a human who painfully grapples with the process of his own thought, and reflects on the problems of the outside world with sensitivity and compassion. Russia's conservative aversion to revolution and pain runs through the idea of compassion and suffering. In a bold statement, prominent conservative Ivan Ilyin notes that 'all Russia's culture is anti-revolutionary and pre-revolutionary'.[12] Hence, the social anthropology of conservative liberals depicts an anti-revolutionary, aloof figure, who is constantly torn, morally and intellectually, between the search for higher justice and happiness for his people and personal abstention, even aesthetic aversion, to the course of history that inevitably throws the masses into suffering, violence and pain in search of such higher goals.

The statist conservative approach, on the other hand, emphasizes the supremacy of the collective over the individual. Pobedonostsev's conviction on this point was clear throughout most of his writings and is indicated in the opening quotation. Those who followed this intellectual path have also been convinced that involvement in the fate of one's people arises from an existential need in all individuals. Without sharing and partaking in the thorny part of one's country, experiencing the pain of its people, a person is reduced to an atomized unit, an uprooted plant dying out and morally degrading without experiencing a higher existential purpose. The main sin of humanity, in their eyes, is the persistent juxtaposition of the individual and the commune (and later community) and the struggle against the supra-individual sources of human history.

State

The contemporary Russian state finds itself in the condition of epistemological uncertainty. It balances between these two approaches and acts as an arbiter. Following a conservative position in general, it appropriates ideas from both branches and attempts to build a reconciliatory ideological position. The state's main goal is to encourage the consolidation of Russia's historic and contemporary narratives. Linking the three separate stages of Russia's history – pre-revolutionary, Soviet and post-Soviet – remains the chief endeavour of Putin's government on the ideological front. In other words, two of Russia's greatest upheavals of the twentieth century (the October 1917 Revolution and the fall of Communism) must be reassessed through the prism of the Russian tradition.

Given that the state in Russia has always been highly personified, the ideological outlook of President Vladimir Putin is a key consideration for this chapter. While some of his economic policies could be appropriated by the liberals, Putin's metaphysical, geopolitical and civilizational stand is clearly conservative. Yet, being both product and leader of his time, Putin balances between the two extant conservative directions. In his annual Addresses to the Federal Assembly, an occasion during which he outlines his vision for the country's immediate economic and political future, Putin alternates between citing the classics of liberal and statist conservative thought – Berdyaev, Ilyin, Losev, and the like. Putin's active support of all

Russia's main religions – Orthodoxy, Islam, Judaism, and Buddhism – falls in line with Russia's modernist conservative preference and her rejection of the postmodernist value package discussed earlier. Yet, even in his religious policies, Putin's balancing between the two branches of Russia's conservatism remains. Putin's presiding over the reunification of the Russian Orthodox Church Abroad and the Russian Orthodox Church was a clear attempt to marry the liberal conservative sentiment of the former with the statist leanings of the latter. Putin's dialogue with the Russian Orthodox Old Believers Church represents a nod in a direction of the most devout statist conservatism.

The enormity of the task of ideological reassessment is also seen in the fact that the Russian public seeks an answer to the question as to what type of conservatism is the most appropriate for the country's development. The public also searches for the ideological values that such conservatism could entail. Bearing in mind that conservatism is often considered as a positionist, rather than ideational, ideology, the pitfalls of this approach lie in accepting this thought as mere anti-liberalism or anti-revolutionism. From this point of view, contemporary Russian conservatism, much like its nineteenth-century predecessor, experiences existential challenges. It aspires to become an integral platform of the Russian state and society, while struggling to obtain a coherent shape and form.

CHAPTER ELEVEN

Conservatism in Japan: Dealing with discontinuity

Christian Winkler

How will many Japanese reply, if asked, 'how did Japan come into being?' Some will bring up the creation of the country told by myth, others will say [it all began] with the ascension to the throne by the first Emperor Jimmu at the palace in Kashihara as told in the Nihon Shoki [Chronicles of Japan, completed in 720 A.D.]. Some will say [. . .] Japan came into being shortly before the times of Prince Shōtoku [an influential member of the Imperial family who lived from 574–622]. In any case, while it is not exactly clear when Japan came into being, we all think that Japan has an extremely long history that continues to this very day. I believe almost all Japanese realize this in how ever vague a fashion. However, this common sense of most Japanese is entirely rejected by the explanation of the Constitution of Japan. I think this is the biggest problem [with the constitution]. The Constitution of Japan explains the creation of Japan as follows: In August 1945, when the theoretical [foundation] of this Constitution was laid, or in 1946, when the constitution was actually drafted, or in 1947, when it came into effect, 'the people of the time have created a new country called Japan by signing a social contract.'

In other words, it follows the logic of clearly denying the continuity of the Japanese nation with its extremely long history and [proclaims] the new birth of a Japanese nation whose ties to its past until that point had been cut off. The Constitution of Japan denies the existence of Japan as a historical entity, while being the 'Constitution of Japan'. The long history and traditions of the Japanese nation have been rejected. It explains that a 'new Japan' was created, disconnected from history. This is the Constitution of Japan's greatest defect . . .

The Constitution of Japan has various issues. However, I think this [the disconnect from the past] is still the most important one, the core part of these issues. Unfortunately, there aren't a lot of people who have pointed this out, even though [. . .] this problem is at the root of the various lapses of postwar Japan.[1]

Japanese conservatism is generally associated with the Liberal Democratic Party (LDP), which has been the governing party for all but four years since its foundation in 1955. As discussed elsewhere, attaching the adjective 'conservative' to the LDP without considerable qualification means either reducing 'conservatism' to a label without any history or meaning, or oversimplifying post-war history.[2] The LDP's strong emphasis on regional equality, clientelism and the more or less emphatic embrace of progressive liberal democratic values by many senior party leaders during long stretches of the post-war period are but a few reminders of the challenge to qualify the LDP as 'conservative', in the same way we refer to Edmund Burke or Russell Kirk as 'conservative'.[3] This chapter thus approaches conservatism in Japan by looking at the political thought of representative conservative figures in the country's intelligentsia, specifically academics and literary critics. The goal of this chapter is to show that despite various institutional and historic differences, it is arguably more appropriate to speak of conservatism in Japan than Japanese conservatism. In fact, I would like to argue that differences between this country's conservatism and the political tradition in Western countries are hardly as significant as geographical, historical and cultural differences may lead the reader to suspect.

The translated passage cited earlier is representative of conservative thought, highlighting the conservative insistence on historical continuity and corresponding disdain for radical reforms and revolutions. To Japanese conservatives, the liberal democratic post-war regime which came into being in the immediate aftermath of the Second World War, is precisely such an ill-advised radical reform. At first glance, it may seem paradoxical to have conservatives argue *against* the present constitutional status quo. Instead, we would expect conservatives to uphold the status quo against progressive attempts at strengthening and/or increasing individual human rights, social justice or getting rid of traditions via proposed amendments.

In Japan, the roles are reversed. Since the constitution came into effect in 1947, conservatives have been pushing for an amendment, while progressives led by the Socialist and Communist parties have been the staunchest defenders of the Japanese supreme law. This role-reversal owes itself to both the content and the creation process of the Constitution of Japan (CoJ), which remains unamended to this date.

To understand this conservative grudge about the creation of the Constitution, it is necessary quickly to review modern Japanese history. After the Japanese Empire accepted the Potsdam Declaration and formally surrendered (thereby ending the Second World War) in September 1945, a seven-year occupation period began. Unlike Germany or Austria, the United States alone acted as the occupation authority in Japan, even though the General Headquarters (GHQ) led by Supreme Commander for the Allied Powers (SCAP) General Douglas MacArthur was at least on paper bound by the decisions of the Far Eastern Commission. Dissatisfied with the Japanese government's unwillingness fundamentally to revise the 1889 constitution (The Constitution of the Great Empire of Japan, also known as Meiji Constitution)[4] and to create a liberal democracy underpinned by popular sovereignty and universal suffrage, MacArthur had GHQ draft an amendment proposal. The Americans insisted that the basic elements of this proposal (changing the emperor's role from sovereign to symbol, popular sovereignty, protection of fundamental human rights and pacifism) should be part of Japan's post-war constitution, despite strong resistance from the Japanese government, which feared such radical reforms would bring about 'chaos, confusion and communism'.[5] The drafting of the constitution under and with considerable involvement by the Occupation authorities quickly gave rise to the argument that the CoJ had been forced upon Japan.[6] This version of history, however, ignores the many continuities that exist between pre- and post-war Japan, for example, in the cases of the imperial and family registration systems.[7] In fact, the initial American draft of the CoJ underwent considerable changes based on input from the Japanese side during the negotiations that followed the submission of this draft to the Japanese government. For instance, certain human rights were limited to Japanese citizens and the National Diet remained a bicameral parliament (as opposed to the unicameral parliament initially proposed by the Americans).[8]

This raises the question of why conservatives focus so strongly on change and historical discontinuities. After all, the Meiji Constitution too came into being as the result of significant reforms during the mid-nineteenth century that saw Japan transform itself into a centralized nation state.[9]

Curiously, most conservative intellectuals have hailed that series of reforms, usually referred to in a slightly misleading manner as Meiji Restoration, as a careful and considerate series of reforms reflecting Japan's long history and traditions.[10] As pointed out elsewhere, the main difference in evaluating those two major discontinuities in modern Japanese history is related to the agent of reform. Conservatives criticize the post-war reforms of 1946–48 as an 'ideological import forced upon Japan by the US' at a time when a defeated and occupied Japan was too weak to say 'no'.[11] Not surprisingly, conservatives do not view this foreign lawgiver in the same positive light as Rousseau once did. To them GHQ was merely an unwelcome and ill-wishing outside force bent on severing Japan's links to its past and thereby weakening Japan to ensure it would never pose a threat to US security again. The weapon of choice was the liberal democratic 1947 Constitution and other reforms, that one conservative intellectual has likened to brainwashing an adult and turning him or her into a 12-year-old child ignorant of his or her proud family history and traditions.[12] In contrast, conservatives praise the Meiji-era political framework as the result of strategic, independent, considerate and historically rooted reforms by Japanese leaders *themselves*.[13]

Apart from the nationalist critique of the foreign lawgiver, the aforementioned criticism of the CoJ's creation out of a historical tabula rasa is hardly uniquely Japanese. After all, the idea goes against not one, but many key features of the conservative political tradition such as the extra-human origins of social order and the preference for organic change. Arguments made by Japanese conservatives are similar to conservative critiques in the West, such as Roger Scruton's criticism of the then British prime minister Tony Blair's 'progressive' constitutional reform initiatives.[14]

The belief in an organic social order, which may not have found expression in a constitution until a later stage of history, but whose manifestations such as traditions and laws shape a constitution is evident in both, Yagi's criticism of the CoJ and Scruton's claim that liberals were quick to forget the continuity of British influences that had helped shape the US Constitution.[15] The rejection of throwing those legal and social traditions out of the window is precisely the same critique that Burke brought forth in what remains arguably conservatism's most influential writing, his *Reflections on the Revolution in France* (1790). As Burke put it, addressing a young gentleman across the channel: 'you had all these advantages in your ancient states, but you chose to act as if you had never been molded into civil society and had everything to begin anew. You began ill, because you began by despising everything that belonged to you. You set up your trade without a capital.'[16] One hundred fifty years after Burke, Oakeshott formulated a similar, yet less blunt, critique of what he called a rationalist '*tabula rasa*' in *Rationalism in Politics and Other Essays*.[17]

Yagi's argument above is identical: Be it out of respect for what previous generations had built or because of man's imperfections the accumulated wisdom of the past and its embodiment in traditions and laws is too precious to discard. Unfortunately, this was exactly what had happened in 1947, when the post-war constitution came into effect. It is hardly surprising then that Japanese conservative intellectuals frequently refer to G. A. Chesterton's 'democracy of the dead'.[18] In his 2004 constitutional amendment proposal, Nishibe makes this 'voting right' of the previous generations explicit, when suggesting that 'on the occasion of the citizens making a decision regarding [the Emperor's] position and its function, [the people] shall accept the limitations stemming from Japanese traditions'.[19]

Radical breaks with established social and legal norms always had negative consequences. While in France, the revolution quickly consumed its children, the negative consequences of the then new constitution and other Occupation-era reforms took more time to show themselves, but as one conservative thinker remarked, '60 years on, Japan no longer has any true elite left and the nation has been weakened'. One small difference to note here is that the French revolutionaries had not anticipated or planned the Reign of Terror in 1789. In Japan in 1946, however, conservatives allege, the United States knew exactly what damage it could do to the Japanese nation and why.[20]

The underlying ideological struggle is reminiscent of the centuries-old battle between conservatives and their progressive foes in Europe, for the Social Contract not only underpinned the creation of the constitution, but liberal thought similar to that of Social Contract icons Locke or Rousseau had also strongly influenced the law's content. This is evident from the fact that the Constitution of Japan has been among the most specific constitutions in enumerating individual rights.[21] The constitution proclaims these fundamental human rights to be 'inherent, inviolable and universal', and by taking cues from the American Constitution, declares, 'all people shall be respected as individuals. Their right to life, liberty, and the pursuit of happiness shall, to the extent that it does not interfere with the public welfare, be the supreme consideration in legislation and other governmental affairs.' Furthermore, 'marriage shall be based only the mutual consent of both sexes,' and laws pertaining to marriage and family 'shall be enacted from the standpoint of individual dignity and the essential equality of the sexes'.[22]

Conservatives have long complained about the liberal individualism underpinning these key stipulations of the Japanese supreme law. Yagi has blamed this 'excessive individualism' and the lack of protection of the (traditional) family in Articles 13 and 24 for an increase in divorces and youth crimes.[23] Nishio does not go quite that far, but notes that we will never know whether people living under the patriarchal pre-war system were really unhappy, and suggests that despite being freed from those chains of traditions and intermediate organizations like the family, present-day Japanese still are far from being happy; instead, frustration was on the rise.[24] Against this backdrop Yagi concluded that 'the grand experiment of individualism' had already failed in the West.[25] Here, we see the conservative link to the past: Conservatives allege that man had gained little from severing ties with Japan's proud history and traditions in 1946. Hence, it is not surprising that Yagi is not alone in advocating the inclusion of a stipulation protecting the family as the basic unit of society in order to strengthen this vital intermediate organization.[26]

Needless to say, the criticism of the liberal quest to free the individual from the yoke of traditions has been a key feature of conservatism on both sides of the Atlantic. In Robert Nisbet's words, 'the conservative philosophy was born of Burke's and others' antagonism to the deadly *etatisme* and *individualisme* which had, like pincers, threatened to crush the traditional intermediate groups in the social order.'[27]

In the early 1980s, Russell Kirk wrote, 'Japanese conservatism, now recovering from the injuries inflicted by war and military occupation, is an interesting development, arising out of the old Japanese concepts of piety, duty and honor. [. . .] Japan wears successively and perhaps sincerely a series of Western masks; but these are discarded in turn, for beneath the masks the old Japanese character lives.'[28]

I would argue that the opposite is also true. As has been pointed out elsewhere,[29] Japanese conservatism has often been defined by its outside appearance, specifically the focus on certain major issues such as the aforementioned constitutional amendment or patriotic education. However, this mask of very specific policy agenda items too frequently hides core principles which Japanese conservatives share with their Western counterparts. Based on different historical realities, Yagi's emphasis on Japan's long history or Etō's praise for eighteen-century conservatism in feudal Japan may be distinct from Voegelin or Kirk's praise for the Middle Ages in Europe. However, the yearning for historical continuity, the belief in the imperfection of man and the resulting necessity for laws and traditions is a commonality. One could discount this commonality as coincidence, if it were not for the strong influence of Western conservatism. Even more than Chesterton or Oakshott, Burke is frequently quoted and his arguments employed by Japanese conservatives who warn of the negative effects of the individual's atomization and rejection of the past, just as Burke had warned his readers about the futility and dangers inherent in the French Revolution.

CHAPTER TWELVE

Conservatism in Europe – the political thought of Christian Democracy

Martin Steven

The reshaping of our economic order had to work towards two things: to bring to an end this division, which hampered progressive development, and to end with it ill-feeling between rich and poor. I do not wish to hide either the material or the moral foundations of my struggle. They determine my actions now as then ... The danger of limitation of competition threatens constantly from many sides. One of the most important tasks in a country based on a free social order is, therefore, to secure free competition. It is no exaggeration when I declare that a law against monopoly is essential as an indispensable 'economic principle'. Should the State fail here, there would be an early end to the 'social market economy'. This principle means that no individual citizen must be powerful enough to suppress individual freedom, or, in the name of false freedom, to be able to limit it. 'Prosperity for all' and 'Prosperity through Competition' are inseparable. The former marks the aim, the latter the path leading to it. These few remarks already show the fundamental difference

*between the social market economy and the liberal economy of
the old days. Businessmen who believe that because of modern
economic developments they can demand cartels are like those
Social Democrats who conclude that automation inevitably leads
to State control. This reflection should shed light on my theory
that it is infinitely more useful to increase prosperity by expansion
than to try for a different distribution of the national income by
pointless quarrelling.*[1]

Ludwig Erhard (1897–1977) is a key figure in the post-war history of
European Christian Democracy. As the West German minister for economic
affairs (1949–63) he is credited with a central role in the divided country's
revival after the devastating conflict of 1939–45. He was not given to explicit
declarations of principle, but this was typical of Christian Democratic
politicians who achieved notable electoral success after the Second World
War in Austria, the Netherlands, Belgium and Italy as well as West Germany
(where the Christian Democratic Union [CDU] continued to hold office
after reunification in 1990). Surprisingly, in view of its importance to an
understanding of post-war European history, the academic literature
on Christian Democracy in English is thin, especially in relation to its
ideological identity.[2] However, European Christian Democratic parties are
invariably characterized as movements on the 'centre right', and they are
usually designated as 'conservative' in nature. Their preference for practical
activity over theoretical speculation can itself be regarded as a characteristic
feature of conservative politics. Indeed, this unexciting profile – 'pragmatic,
centrist but distinctively conservative' – might help to explain the relative
lack of academic interest.[3]

The title of Erhard's book *Prosperity through Competition* (1959) from
which the above extract is taken provides a clear indication of the Christian
Democratic approach to economic matters, which in turn epitomizes a more
general approach to social and political questions. After suffering serious
wounds as an officer in the First World War, Erhard had studied economics
at the University of Frankfurt, later working in the Nüremberg Business
School. He was associated with a group of economists (mainly based at
the University of Freiburg), who championed the free market, rather than
an economy subjected to excessive state intervention. This viewpoint (later
dubbed 'ordoliberalism') envisaged an important role for the state, in
particular to prevent the creation of private monopolies. The state, therefore,
should be strong enough to ensure free competition through regulation; it
should act as a 'referee' rather than one of the players on the pitch, taking
impartial decisions in the national interest.[4] This was far removed from the
Nazi vision of the state, and it was surprising that Erhard was allowed to

retain his academic post until 1942. His record and his beliefs made him an ideal consultant for the allied armies of occupation after the war, and Erhard remained a powerful figure in West German politics for the next two decades.

What Erhard and his advisors dubbed the 'social market' (*soziale marktwirtschaft*) approach was well suited to the task of post-war reconstruction because it was designed to foster harmony within economic enterprises. It was characteristic of Erhard to dismiss the symptoms of industrial conflict as 'pointless quarrelling' – Erhard, indeed, regarded partisan politics in much the same light, and did not formally join the CDU until 1963 when he was about to succeed Konrad Adenauer as West German chancellor.[5] Among other measures to promote cooperation in industry, Christian Democracy encouraged the participation of workers' representatives on the boards of private companies. The approach also had important ramifications for social policy. The prosperity generated by private industry would be used by the state to provide for those who were in no position to support themselves.

This general approach envisaged the state as a promoter of partnership – a supporter of social and economic 'consensus'. This is widely recognized as a key conservative aim, lending itself to stability. However, prior to 1945, German conservatism had been associated with a different approach to such questions, in which the state (preferably under a restored monarchy) would underpin a relatively rigid social hierarchy dominated by landed aristocrats. In sharp contrast, the policy framework indicated by the CDU's social market was designed to facilitate freedom within civil society, guaranteed by democratic principles enshrined in the constitution (or 'Basic Law') promulgated in 1949. In the same year, the Christian Democrat Konrad Adenauer (1876–1967) became West Germany's first post-war chancellor.

Adenauer's previous career provides useful insights into the nature of German Christian Democracy. Unlike Erhard he was a 'career politician', having served as mayor of Cologne between 1917 and 1933 – crucial years for Germany, in which the country struggled to establish a liberal democracy after defeat in the First World War, then succumbed to the Nazi dictatorship. Adenauer had already shown a propensity for constructive cooperation with political opponents in the interests of stability. However, he was identified as a likely opponent of the Nazis and lost his political offices when Hitler came to power. Under Hitler's tyranny he was in constant danger and was imprisoned more than once. Adenauer was a devout Roman Catholic, and had represented the faith-based Centre Party during his early career. However, he had never implemented sectarian policies, and after the war he worked for a realignment of the various Christian movements in the interests of political stability. His association with Ludwig Erhard – a Bavarian Lutheran – illustrated his ecumenical approach. As befitted their contrasting backgrounds, the two men were very different characters who personified underlying tensions between 'conservative' and 'liberal' approaches to governance: while Adenauer had no principled objection to state intervention when he judged this to be necessary, Erhard (as the above extract shows) had an inbuilt bias in favour of economic freedom.[6] But during the crucial post-war years, they kept their differences under wraps, in pursuit of their common understanding of the national interest.

Thus, the West German CDU could hardly have adopted a more informative name. It originated in long-established Christian political movements, and continued to draw strong support from the main German faith groups. But this 'Union' of Christians hoped that religion could both symbolize and cement a social consensus in a Germany which worked within democratic institutions carefully crafted to protect freedom of religious conscience, among other liberties. The party was therefore 'Christian' and 'Democratic'; but was it distinctively 'conservative'?

If the CDU were to be judged on the outlook of its founding leader, its conservative credentials would be unequivocal. Adenauer frequently gave voice to sentiments which betrayed a highly pessimistic (even cynical) view of human nature. ('In view of the fact that God limited the intelligence of man, it seems unfair that He did not also limit his stupidity.'[7]) More importantly, Adenauer's outlook – and that of the CDU in general – was informed by a respect for tradition which is highly characteristic of conservatives. The German experience since the fall of Bismarck in 1890 had been punctuated by spectacular upheavals. But the ill-starred Weimar Republic (1919–33) had been one of several attempts to establish liberal constitutions, from which valuable lessons could be absorbed by conservatives. Bismarck himself had presided over the establishment of a pioneering system of state welfare; and the idea of partnership between labour and capital in the workplace had been endorsed by Pope Leo XIII in his encyclical *Rerum Novarum* (1891).

Thus, in the early post-war years, the West German CDU could be seen as perfectly acceptable by moderate liberals, and highly congenial for those who regarded themselves as 'conservative'. Many of the latter had sided either tacitly or openly with Hitler. For them, the CDU offered an excellent chance for a fresh start – a way of 'de-Nazifying' themselves through identification with politicians who had never collaborated, and beginning the process of cleansing their country's reputation. In simplistic electoral terms, the CDU squared the democratic circle – its conservatism could draw support from rural areas, Erhard's free-market ideas were sure to appeal to ambitious entrepreneurs and the 'social market' approach could attract workers as well as the representatives of big business who were prepared to tolerate Erhard's animosity towards monopolistic practices in return for the prospect of harmonious labour relations.

If the CDU's appeal within West Germany owed much to its 'conservative' elements, for external observers its value derived crucially from its promise of stability in the context of ideological confrontation between the democratic West and the Soviet-dominated East. Although the party stood for a compromise between free-market liberalism on the American model and bureaucratic dictation along Soviet lines, its stance was appropriate for a state which was oriented towards the West. It was, in short, resolutely anti-Communist, although it was careful not to increase the existing tensions between the Cold War antagonists. This external dimension was, of course, an important ingredient in the success of Christian Democrat parties in other European countries.

Christian Democracy in practice

For a conservative, not even the most attractive statement of principles can rival the importance of practical success – in other words, the establishment of 'governing competence'. In post-war liberal democracies the key measure of success has been economic prosperity. By 1959, when Ludwig Erhard published the book quoted earlier, Christian Democrats in West Germany and elsewhere could claim to have passed this test. West Germany itself was recognized as the beneficiary of an 'economic miracle' (*Wirtshaftswunder*) through the application of Erhard's ideas.

Indeed, from the viewpoint of politicians who were acutely concerned with European stability it could easily appear that West Germany's social market approach was proving too successful for comfort. Despite constitutional provisions designed to guard against a military resurgence, it was understandable that the state's neighbours (and their American allies) should feel unsettled by the prospect of economic domination. The CDU's answer to this problem was to sponsor proposals for European unity, leading to the establishment of the European Economic Community (EEC) under the Treaty of Rome (1957). While other politicians (notably Charles de Gaulle and Margaret Thatcher: see Chapters 14 and 16) might have regarded the EEC as at best a necessary nuisance, for the CDU close cooperation (hopefully leading to outright political union) tended to be regarded as something akin to an ideological principle. Although Erhard and Adenauer had different visions for Europe – the latter prioritized West Germany's relationship with France, while Erhard had stronger Atlanticist leanings – they both rejected crude inter-war German nationalism. Rather, these feelings should be diverted into a more constructive channel – a sense of national pride which was fully consistent with the pooling of West Germany's resources with its European partners.

The extent to which the CDU succeeded in 'civilizing' nationalistic feeling in West Germany is reflected in attitudes towards the territorial division imposed after 1945. A succession of CDU-dominated governments focused on the fortunes of their own citizens in the West, while keeping the possibility of reunification alive by maintaining amicable relations with the Soviets and their satellite states (a pragmatic approach known as *Ostpolitik*). In 1990, the dream was finally realized, under a Christian Democrat–dominated government led by Helmut Kohl (1930–2017), a Roman Catholic from the Rhineland. Kohl also worked closely with the socialist French president Francois Mitterand on a programme to deepen European integration, which culminated in the declaration of a European Union in the Maastricht Treaty signed in 1992.

Christian Democracy in decay?

From the vantage point of 1992, German Christian Democracy could easily seem like an unalloyed success story. The CDU's absorption of liberal economics within a framework of ideas which also featured distinctively conservative elements seemed to have taken the country from division to reconciliation at a variety of levels. The significant exception to the general welcome of reunification – the United Kingdom's Margaret Thatcher – actually reinforced that lesson, since her blend of strident nationalism and aggressive championship of the free market made her a natural antagonist of the conservatism of Christian Democracy.

However, the inherent ideological tensions incorporated within the CDU's 'liberal–conservative' approach had already been exposed, at least in part thanks to its practical success. In the terminology of political science, the CDU had been established as a 'catch-all' party, offering a tepid ideological brew which only satisfied politicians and voters who accepted that this was the best that could be expected in unpropitious post-war circumstances.[8] When Erhard succeeded Adenauer as West German chancellor in 1963, he had been troubled by the emergence of a 'consumerist' ethos which threatened to undermine feelings of national solidarity. Erhard was particularly worried by the strength of West German interest groups, notably the trade unions. At the CDU's 1965 party conference he drew on the recent work of the conservative theorist Rüdiger Altmann, and referred to the idea of an 'aligned society' (*formierte Gesellschaft*). Radical critics, who already regarded Christian Democracy as an instrument of the West German middle class, accused Erhard of trying to use the power of the state to exclude dissident voices – in short, of trying to preserve a pretence of economic pluralism, while resorting to political authoritarianism.[9] The idea of the 'aligned society' was quickly dropped, and Erhard himself was forced from office in 1966.

Although the CDU recovered from this existential emergency, it could not afford to rest on its laurels in the aftermath of the Cold War, and faced the challenge of (at least) presenting its tried and trusted electoral offering in new packaging. The problem was more acute for other Christian Democratic parties which had succeeded at the ballot box, but whose practical achievements were less palpable. Too often, the senior ranks of these parties were dominated by colourless technocrats, drawn to political activism not by earnest convictions of any kind, but rather by an interest in problem-solving – or by a desire for personal gain. The end of the Cold War exposed the extent to which individuals in the latter category had infiltrated European Christian Democratic parties. The most notorious example of this phenomenon was Italy, whose *Democrazia Cristiana* (DC) party collapsed in 1994, after five decades of dominance, amid accusations of corruption which engulfed senior figures as well as lesser functionaries. Then again, the DC had always operated within a political culture in which corrupt practices of various kinds had been prevalent, and which offered far less scope for political stability than other European states; its eventual fate was only delayed until a time when it was safe to publicize its activities. It was more surprising that Kohl himself incurred considerable unpopularity during his last term in office (1994–8), and after his resignation his legacy was tainted by revelations concerning illegal donations to the CDU.

While Konrad Adenauer and Ludwig Erhard would have been disconcerted by these developments, they could in fact have been predicted on the basis of their approach to politics in the CDU's early years. Adenauer, with his pessimistic view of human nature, could have no illusions about the tendency of power of any kind to corrupt. Erhard, in the extract quoted earlier, expressed his vehement opposition to economic monopolies. Exactly the same warning could have been issued in relation to *political* monopolies. As soon as the citizens of any European state could safely conclude that a Christian Democrat party would dominate the next government, regardless of the forthcoming election result, something dangerously akin to the unhealthy results of an economic monopoly were bound to ensue: the consumer (or, in this case, the voter) would always be the loser in the final analysis. In this respect, when Adenauer and Erhard helped to found a party which was designed to appeal to the maximum proportion of West German voters, they were running the risk that they were sowing the seeds of their own destruction.

Thus, after the end of the Cold War, the future of Christian Democracy was in serious doubt unless politicians who identified with that tradition proved equal to the challenges of a new era. In this task they faced a handicap which had not affected Adenauer or Erhard in the late 1940s. Throughout Europe, attendance at Christian services of any denomination had fallen consistently since 1945; and the trend has not been markedly different in countries, such as Germany, which still provide considerable electoral support to parties claiming the 'Christian Democrat' label. Since 2005, Germany's chancellor has been Helmut Kohl's protégée, Angela Merkel. As the daughter of a Lutheran clergyman, whose early years were spent in East Germany before reunification, Merkel is in herself a tribute to the continuing appeal of Christian Democracy despite the disappearance of its original Cold War context. Yet it can be argued that her longevity in office is a testament to her considerable political abilities rather than a reflection of the popularity of the tradition of political thinking with which she identifies.

Even if Christian Democracy no longer excites many Germans, Merkel has continued to be a potent symbol of success and stability.

In summary, it is tempting to designate European Christian Democracy as a phenomenon which marked a specific moment in time. On this view, the Second World War created a context in which centre-right political parties recognized the importance of a platform that could rally conservative voters without alienating their more radical opponents, thereby winning democratic elections but, more importantly, coming as close as possible to generating a national 'consensus' wherever Christian Democrats were a potent force. This desire to rebuild stable polities on the basis of a ubiquitous Christian heritage, combined with hopes of a more prosperous future based on an acceptance of the liberal post-war economy backed by American fire-power, could look very persuasive on paper in the circumstances of 1945, and was capable of securing acquiescence (at least). Although the example of the CDU could easily be misleading given the unique circumstances of West Germany in the years between the war and the country's reunification, it would be reasonable to argue on the basis of that experience that politicians like Ludwig Erhard and Konrad Adenauer could use the principles of Christian Democracy in a way which would satisfy all but the most purist of conservatives, offering a genuine semblance of social and political harmony rather than an enforced stability. However, even in Germany, where Christian Democrats can point to so many significant historic achievements, the conservative–liberal approach to politics had begun to show signs of strain even in the 1960s, and now seems unduly dependent on the fortunes on a single individual. In the elections of 2017, it was all too easy to portray Merkel as the representative of a conservative variant whose time was running out, in the face of insurgents from both the left and a newly invigorated right which was uninhibited by attempts to associate it with the most inglorious episodes of Germany's part.[10]

CHAPTER THIRTEEN

Conservatism in Turkey

Bekir Varoglu, Mark Garnett and Simon Mabon

The Justice and Development Party (AK Party) is a conservative democratic mass party that situates itself at the center of the political spectrum . . .
According to our notion of conservative democracy, the realm of politics is based on a culture of compromise. The articulation of societal differences in the realm of politics can only become possible if politics are founded on a basis of compromise. Societal and cultural diversity should participate in politics on the foundation of democratic pluralism produced by tolerance and allowance . . . Conservative democracy which is in favor of limited and defined political government views totalitarian and authoritarian approaches as enemies of democratic politics. Conservative democracy values political legitimacy based on the will of the people and the common values of humanity . . .
The concept of the rule of law, albeit couched in Western philosophy, necessitates limiting governments and institutions according to objective rules and laws emanating from universal values . . . Conservative democracy is based on an understanding that favours gradual and phased change over top-down change.

Societal change is the most fundamental and durable form of change. Interrupting socio-economic, cultural and political life is negative as it abrogates accumulated knowledge, experience and historical development . . .
AK Party does not view conservatism as being opposed to change. Rather, it defines conservatism as being opposed to authoritarian and radical change. It has thus completed 'silent revolutions' based on an understanding of gradual change and societal dynamics.[1]

When evaluating the principles of any political movement as opposed to individual thinkers, students of ideology almost invariably face the challenge of teasing out the implicit or underlying meanings of texts which have been produced to meet a variety of exigencies. The above excerpt seems to be a notable exception. It makes an explicit ideological claim on behalf of a movement, expounds the principles of that ideology and sets out its practical implications in a specific national context. One is tempted to think that the excerpt needs no further comment in this volume: if you need a concise illustration of conservatism in Turkey, here it is. However, on closer inspection, the passage provides far more questions than answers, and demands an interesting variation in the usual process of ideological analysis.

The excerpt is taken from a document, published in September 2012, entitled *Political Vision of the AK Parti (Justice and Development Party)*, as part of a wide-ranging programme for Turkey in the years running up to the Republic's centenary in 2023. Among the objectives set out by the AK Parti (better known outside Turkey as the AKP) – the ruling party in Turkey since winning a majority in the legislative elections of 2002 – was membership of the European Union (EU), for which the country had originally applied in 1987. In 2012, it was pursuing this goal with greater vigour, and had established links with the EU's main centre-right grouping, the European People's Party (EPP). It was thus no accident that the document quoted earlier advocates a mode of a conservatism which is broadly comparable to that of mainstream European Christian Democratic parties, incorporating several ideas more usually associated with liberal ideology.[2] It stresses the AKP's commitment to diversity, tolerance and compromise: to the rule of law, and democratic practices 'based on the will of the people and the common values of humanity'.[3] The party also advocates 'limited' government, and a free-market economy. However, these objectives are qualified in a fashion which also echoes the approach of Christian Democratic parties, notably the German CDU (see Chapter 12); the AKP document highlights its record on welfare spending, particularly on education, healthcare and housing, while emphasizing that the state will continue to play a stabilizing role in order to contain the 'savagery of capitalism', albeit as 'a facilitator rather than a force preventing creativity and development' (*AKP*, 32–47).

Thus, in its philosophy and its practical programme, the AKP was offering the kind of formula which in most European states would undoubtedly place it on the centre-right, and most commentators in those countries would classify it as a vehicle for modern conservatism. However, while the blend of liberalism and conservatism provided a basis for electoral success and governing competence in Germany and elsewhere, in the Turkish context the inherent tensions in the formula seemed more problematic. Apart from the usual virtues claimed by conservatives – the advocacy of piecemeal rather than radical reform, the emphasis on social cohesion, and the like – the document also promises that the party will rely on 'accumulated knowledge, experience and historical development'. This sits awkwardly with the endorsement of 'universal values' which are acknowledged to derive from 'Western philosophy'. The attentive reader would be entitled to ask how these abstract concepts would translate into the Turkish context. Five years after the publication of the document, that question was still awaiting an authoritative answer.

Conservatism and 'Kemalism'

The issue of context prompts a comparison between the AKP's statement of principle and the ideas of Mustafa Kemal Ataturk (1881–1938), the founder of modern Turkey. As a dynamic movement which claims to promote national unity and purpose, the AKP can certainly be compared to the Republican People's Party, the vehicle for Ataturk's rule. In Recep Tayyip Erdogan (b. 1954) – a one-time footballer and former mayor of Istanbul – the AKP also has a charismatic and forceful leader who is often compared to Ataturk.

However, the parallels between the two movements are less instructive than the contrasts. In particular, Ataturk's answer to the problem of context was a concerted effort to erase any differences between Turkey and liberal democracies in the West. In particular, Ataturk was antipathetic to the religion of Islam – an issue which has played a crucial part in public and private life since the days of the Ottoman Empire. Ataturk was reported to have remarked that 'I have no religion, and at times I wish all religions at the bottom of the sea.'[4] Erdogan, by sharp contrast, was brought up as a devout Muslim and became the mayor of Istanbul as the candidate of the Islamic Welfare Party. This organization was subsequently banned by the Turkish Constitutional Court; Erdogan himself was excluded from political life and briefly imprisoned in 1997, after incorporating in one of his speeches lines from a pro-Islamic poem.[5]

A case could be made for incorporating Ataturk himself within a broad tradition of 'conservative' governance. On this view, he regarded Islam as not only an obstacle to the desired modernization of Turkey, but also as a likely source of political and social instability. After the collapse of the Ottoman Empire and the disastrous outcome of the First World War, Ataturk believed that Turkey could only survive as a viable entity if it was reconstructed as a strictly secular state.[6]

However, this argument is unpersuasive even after a cursory analysis of Ataturk's attitudes and actions. On the 'conservative' reading, Ataturk could be viewed as a pragmatist who took the necessary steps to drag his country into the twentieth century. However, there is good evidence to suggest that Ataturk was strongly attracted by liberal rationalism in principle as well as in practice. This explains his willingness to adopt methods which were reminiscent of the French revolutionaries. In his *Reflections on the French Revolution*, Edmund Burke asserted that 'man is by his constitution a religious animal; that atheism is against, not only our reason but our instincts; and that it cannot prevail long'.[7] From this perspective, Burke ranked the attempts of French revolutionaries to extirpate Catholicism high among their numerous offences (see Chapter 5).

In 1924, the year after Ataturk became Turkey's president, references to Islam (previously recognized as the state religion) were excised from the constitution. Dress, education, working practices, even the calendar and the alphabet were subjected to sweeping 'Westernizing' reforms.[8] Far from seeking a way to preserve some respect for his country's political traditions, as a conservative would be expected to do, Ataturk sought to supersede them and to erase memories of the Ottoman Empire. Even Ataturk's adopted name symbolizes his distance from the conservative outlook – to allow oneself to be called 'Father of the Turks' is to accept the unconservative view that a nation's life can begin with the rule of a single individual.

While Ataturk presented himself as the embodiment of an ideology – Kemalism – the AKP document of 2012 portrays the party as a movement whose appeal derives from the cogency and coherence of its ideas rather than association with any political figure. The AKP's reaction against Ataturk is most obvious in its stated objections to authoritarian, 'top-down' change. Echoing Burke, the document insists that conservatism should not be confused with last-ditch defence of the status quo, but that reform should emerge from an organic process based on respect for tradition.

On this basis, if Ataturk was 'Father of the Turks', the AKP's document presents it as 'The Party of the Turks' – a 'catch-all' party in the parlance of political science, again reminiscent of the German Christian Democratic Union. A more sober appraisal of the AKP's project would begin with the argument that Ataturk's secularism has proved unsuitable for Turkey, and that this was entirely predictable from a conservative viewpoint. Islam, and memories of the Ottomans, were far too potent to be repressed out of existence. Despite Ataturk's efforts, Islam retained the allegiance of an overwhelming majority of Turks. The cultural legacy of the Ottoman Empire proved equally enduring, remaining highly visible (for example) in the architecture of Istanbul (the former Constantinople), in contrast to Ankara which became the Republic's capital under Ataturk.

The AKP document suggests a desire to learn from Ataturk's mistakes rather than to emulate his example by attempting to efface his acknowledged achievement in transforming the country from the nineteenth century's 'sick man of Europe' to a significant power on the global stage. The obvious way to move on from Kemalism was to show that Islam can play a constructive role within a Turkish state and society which nevertheless continues to exhibit significant similarities with Western democracies. This interpretation explains the 2012 AKP document's reference to 'Societal and cultural diversity'. On the one hand, this could be read as a signal to Muslims that the state will no longer discriminate against them – and, indeed, that the majority Sunni population would not repress other denominations. Equally, it offers reassurance to non-Muslims at home – and Western governments – that the secular state will not be replaced by some kind of theocracy, in which the discriminatory boot will henceforth be on the other foot.

In the quoted document, the AKP's approach is hailed as a model for other countries in the region to follow in the wake of the numerous popular uprisings (the 'Arab Spring') which began in 2011. Change in neighbouring countries, the document stressed, was inevitable; but 'it must take place peacefully and with national consensus' (*AKP* 2012, 64). However, the practical application of the AKP's ideas to contemporary Turkey, let alone the wider region, was always likely to raise difficulties. The removal of 'Kemalist' restrictions on devout followers of Islam could easily inspire attempts to reclaim the privileged position which Islam enjoyed under the Ottomans, influencing state policy and transforming intermediate institutions such as education and the law. The 'top-down' Kemalist programme, in short, might be sent into reverse. In turn, this would expose the extent to which Ataturk had actually *succeeded* in his drive to transform Turkish society and culture. A substantial proportion of the Turkish people has embraced secularism; opinion surveys suggest that more than 10 per cent of Turks have no religious affiliation, and even many of those who retain their Islamic faith are disinclined to welcome even the hint of theocracy.[9] Thus, an approach which was clearly designed to appeal to all Turks, whether secular or religious, could very easily end up exposing and accentuating thinly concealed divisions.

The AKP in practice

The foregoing interpretation derives support from the course of events since the publication of the quoted document in 2012. In June 2013, Germany blocked talks on Turkey's accession to the EU after Erdogan's government responded violently to a protest held in Istanbul's Taksim Square – a place with strong historical resonances relating to the Ottoman

Empire as well as commemorating the foundation of the Republic.[10] In November 2013, the AKP broke off its relationship with the EPP and allied itself to a Eurosceptic grouping in the European Parliament, signaling that Erdogan's government was now far less interested in EU membership. At least in part, the new tougher line against dissent was inspired by clear evidence which contradicted the 2012 document's distinctively conservative claim that under AKP governance 'Turkey is making peace with its own history and geography' (AKP 2012, 65). This implied a concerted attempt to bring a peaceful end to the long-running campaign to secure independence for Turkey's Kurish population in the south of the country, but in practice Erdogan resumed the more familiar tactic of violent repression.[11]

Under Attaturk and his successors, the Turkish military had enjoyed a degree of popularity and influence which was difficult to reconcile with a healthy liberal democracy. However, Erdogan had obvious reasons to resent the armed forces, which portrayed themselves as guarantors of the secular republic. Once the AKP had won power, he began to promote AKP supporters in place of Kemalist officers. In July 2016, a group within the military attempted a coup, essentially arguing that the conservative principles stated by the AKP in 2012 had proved to be a sham. Instead, Ataturk's secular regime was being undermined, democracy was endangered and human rights were being abused. The attempt was quickly suppressed; and in its wake hundreds of thousands of people – known dissidents, soldiers, teachers and journalists – were either imprisoned or dismissed.[12]

The abortive coup was so convenient for Erdogan that many were ready to believe that he had either planned or at least encouraged it himself. The fact that this interpretation was widely believed is in itself a reflection on the AKP's self-proclaimed 'conservatism', since the self-interested promotion of instability must be counted as the most culpable of conservative sins. Suspicions grew when Erdogan called a referendum on constitutional proposals which essentially envisaged a switch from parliamentary to presidential government. Despite a very favourable context, in the poll (April 2017), the government prevailed by a narrow margin, and international observers were not satisfied that it had been fairly conducted. No democrat could have regarded a vote of just over 50% as decisive in such momentous decisions; a conservative would have taken it as the signal for the kind of compromise recommended in the 2012 AKP document. Erdogan, however, was in no mood to cut a deal with his critics.

The wheel has not turned a complete circle in Turkey, and Ataturk is still a respected figure. However, it seems that the coup and the referendum have cemented the position of a regime with comparable power, which is determined to disprove the gist of Ataturk's remark that 'He is a weak ruler who needs religion to uphold his government'.[13] Edmund Burke's notion that religion is an eradicable component of human nature – and his apparent assumption that it lends invariable support to conservative governance – was easily refutable in his own lifetime, from an observation of politics in his native Ireland. If divisions between Christians in the late eighteenth century acted as a driver for intolerant policies and violent resistance, the same considerations may also be true of Islam in the early twenty-first century.[14] Nevertheless, apparently Erdogan is hoping to prove that a state which is Islamic in nature if not (as yet) in name can be stable and prosperous in a globalized economy. It is too early to tell whether his attempt will be successful; but if it does succeed, it will do so on a basis which is far removed from the 'conservative-democratic' position outlined in *Political Vision of the AK Parti.*

It would be perverse, rather than merely ironic, if the AKP had claimed to be 'conservative' only as a tactical ploy to help it secure a position from which it could usher in an indefinite period of violent instability. Nevertheless, this scenario is inherently plausible. After all, the ill-fated Welfare Party which provided Erdogan with his initial power base had a clear ideological mission which could be characterized as 'conservative', but is better described as 'reactionary' since it was inspired at least in part by a romanticized view of the Ottoman Empire. It argued that Islamic states in general had been corrupted by contact with the West and that Turkey could reclaim its leading role in the Islamic world only if it threw off that influence.

In 2001, another explicitly Islamist organization (the 'Virtue' Party') was held by the Constitutional Court to have infringed the state's secular principles.[15] For ambitious Islamicist leaders like Erdogan, the only recourse was to seek power under a different guise. His timing was propitious; the AKP was founded less than a month before the '9/11' terrorist attacks in New York and Washington. A movement which claimed to be 'conservative-democratic' – an identity on which Erdogan continued to insist, as opposed to 'Muslim-democratic' – was far less likely to incur obstruction from the Turkish courts, and to secure a warm welcome from the United States and (especially) the EU.

We saw earlier that the 2012 document exhibited a tension between 'conservative' and 'liberal' elements. It could be argued that since then the AKP has discarded the de-contextualized 'liberalism', while retaining the 'conservative' principles. To some observers, conservatism is synonymous with 'authoritarian' rule; and on this basis Erdogan has merely moved since 2012 from a 'democratic' or 'liberal' style of conservatism to its more usual manifestation.[16] However, as Ataturk's record shows, 'authoritarianism' is not the monopoly of a single ideology. It is most usefully understood as a mode of governance adopted by any regime which seeks to impose uniform obedience on a society which exhibits unmistakable symptoms of a frustrating diversity, and (as in the example of Stalin's misuse of power in the Soviet Union) thus can become an end in itself if the society in question refuses to conform.

For conservatives, repression can only be justified as a temporary measure to bring a nation to its senses – to restore a social harmony which has been disrupted by developments which are alien to its traditional practices.

Erdogan and his supporters presumably view Ataturk's initiatives as an example of such an alien intrusion, and continue to regard themselves as agents of a blessed restoration which will ultimately promote national unity under Islamic guidance. However, the secularist genie cannot be forced back into its bottle. Turkey is a bitterly divided nation state, beset by multiple fault lines – as, indeed, it was throughout the history of the Ottoman Empire, which in its latter stages oscillated between 'liberal' initiatives to embrace 'societal and cultural diversity' and outright genocide (culimating in the Armenian massacres which disgraced the Empire's last decade).

Turkey has never been an exception to the general rule that the strength of identity politics in any state or region bears an inverse relationship to the possibility of 'conservative' governance, in any meaningful sense. In their attempt to recreate an Islamic state in Turkey, Erdogan and the AKP are clearly aware that their hand has been enhanced by the anti-Islamic Ataturk; thanks to his efforts, Turkey is now too strong as well as too extensive and complicated for other global players to contemplate its collapse with equanimity. On current trends, it looks as if a party which promised to prove that political Islam could embrace a 'conservative' brand of pluralism looks set to follow the familiar model of repressive rule in the Middle East, struggling to maintain a veneer of stability in a way which gives additional impetus to Turkey's centrifugal forces.

PART FOUR

Conservatism in practice

CHAPTER FOURTEEN

Gaullism: A personal conservatism

David S. Bell

All my life I have had a certain idea of France. This is inspired as much by sentiment as by reason. What is affective in me tends to imagine France, like the princess in the fairy tale or the Madonna in the frescoes, as dedicated to an exalted and exceptional destiny. Instinctively I have the feeling that Providence has created her either for complete success or for exemplary misfortunes. If, in spite of this, mediocrity shows in her acts and deeds, it strikes me as an absurd anomaly, to be imputed to the faults of Frenchmen, not to the genius of the land. But the positive side of my mind also assures me that France is not really herself unless she is in the front rank; that only vast enterprises are capable of counter-balancing the ferments of dispersion inherent in her people; that our country, as it is, surrounded by the others, such as they are, must aim high and hold itself straight, on pain of mortal danger. In short, to my mind, France cannot be France without grandeur.

This faith grew as I grew, in the environment where I was born. My father was a thoughtful, cultivated, traditional man, imbued

*with the feeling of the dignity of France. He made me aware of
her history. My mother had an uncompromising passion for her
country, equal to her religious piety. To my three brothers, my
sister and myself a certain anxious pride in our country came as
second nature. As a young Lille-born boy living in Paris, nothing
struck me more than the symbols of our glories: night falling over
Notre Dame, the majesty of the evening at Versailles, the Arc de
Triomphe in the sun, conquered colours fluttering in the vault of
the Invalides. Nothing affected me more than the evidence of
our national successes: popular enthusiasm when the Tsar of
Russia passed through, a review at Longchamp, the marvels of
the Exhibition, the flights of our first aviators. Nothing saddened
me more profoundly than our weaknesses and our mistakes,
as revealed to my childhood gaze by the way people looked and
by the things they said: the surrender at Fashoda, the Dreyfus
case, social conflicts, religious strife. Nothing moved me so much
as the story of our past misfortunes: my father recalling the
fruitless sortie from Le Bourget and Stains, in which he had been
wounded; my mother conjuring up the despair she had felt as a
girl at the sight of her parents in tears: 'Bazaine has surrendered.'*[1]

This extract is taken from the famous first page of the *War Memoirs*, published
in French in 1954, of Charles de Gaulle (1890–1970). It is an exercise in
literary style, Chateaubriand-like in its classical elegance; and it sets the
tone for the rest of the work. What is clear is that de Gaulle's conservatism
prioritized the projection of France on the world stage through leadership.
De Gaulle establishes himself as the patriot's patriot, taking the moral high
ground with the mystical exercise in describing France (as the Madonna
of the fairy tales). De Gaulle touches on events and imagery that cover the
spectrum of French political currents but without tying himself to any single
faction. Of course, no Republican would evoke the fairy princesses, but the
reference to Fashoda (where the French and British imperialisms confronted
each other in 1898) coupled with the modernistic references to flying
exploits make it difficult to place: *on ne sort de l'ambiguïté qu'à ses dépens.*
In evoking these images and events, de Gaulle is careful not to comment
on them or to offer a critical review in keeping with his determination to
overcome the divisions that are so debilitating to French life. Most politicians
regard themselves as patriots, but very few can manoeuvre themselves into
the position of representing their country as the embodiment of patriotism.[2]

General de Gaulle was a political figure of the mid-twentieth century but latterly an almost mythical persona as leader of the Free French (1940–44) and subsequently head of the Provisional Government (1944–46). Thus, de Gaulle re-emerged in the French context of national crisis in 1958 with credentials as an '*homme providential*' (or national saviour) that were already established. Unlike many of the conservative centre-right movements in Europe at this time – even Britain, with its cult of Churchill and potent wartime mythology – Gaullism was centred on an individual, but was also patriotic and nationalistic in a very forthright way, and this is a distinguishing feature.

Charles de Gaulle

Charles de Gaulle was born in Lille on 22 November 1890.[3] De Gaulle's father was a school teacher and two of his mother's sisters were nuns. Charles attended military school in Saint-Cyr. As a Catholic, de Gaulle came from a milieu of '*le Ralliement*' – the decision, under papal influence, of intellectual Catholicism to reconcile itself to Republican politics and the parliamentary system. This was also the time of the papal encyclical *Rerum Novarum* and the burgeoning of Catholic social policy.[4] Under Pope Leo XIII, the Church responded to the rise of socialism and liberalism by developing a social theory that anticipated the welfare states and which developed into Christian Democracy in the twentieth century. These ideas of social Catholicism were generous, and influenced de Gaulle's associates who laid the foundations for state insurance, health and working condition regulations after the Second World War. In the First World War, de Gaulle was wounded twice and taken prisoner in March 1916 at the battle of Douaumont. De Gaulle subsequently published a number of articles and books on military strategy and history, urging in particular that the French infantry should enhance its mobility by adopting modern technology, notably tanks. These views were supposedly unwelcome in senior military circles, but proved prophetic when France was exposed to Germany's *blitzkrieg*.[5]

In 1940, de Gaulle quit France after the 16 June armistice to issue from London two days later the famous 'Call to Resistance'. That de Gaulle emerged as the undisputed leader of the Free French is a high tribute to political skills and to his unique brand of leadership. His determination to uphold the dignity of his country, even in defeat, did not endear him to Churchill or Roosevelt. He returned to France as prime minister in 1944 but resigned in January 1946. In 1947, the Rally for France (RPF) was founded to campaign for a new constitution and in defiance of the 'regime of parties' (the Gaullist 'party' was prudently called a 'rally' to avoid the impression of factionalism). This failed to make a breakthrough, and de Gaulle went into retirement until the Algerian war came to a crisis point. Famously, he returned to head the government in the Algerian crisis of May 1958, during which the Fourth Republic's authority had evaporated in the face of an attempted coup by French forces in Algiers.[6] De Gaulle's return to power was thus in part fuelled by a conservative demand for authority and stability in the midst of a turbulent situation which the Fourth Republic had been unable to master.

A French conservatism?

De Gaulle's political views have their place in the French conservative tradition and that defies easy transcription for an English-language audience. Despite the *Ralliement*, conservatives tended to be grudging in their acceptance of Republicanism, or indeed hostile to it. René Rémond's triptych of Bonapartism, Royalist Legitimism and Orleanism catches the essential features of French conservatism.[7] This right wing in France was in part –at least – a disaffected aristocracy and that gave an insurrectionary aspect to some of its movements. Possibly because of the emphasis that Gaullism places on leadership, it was often dismissed as a contemporary version of Bonapartism. In the emphasis on the strong state, leadership and the necessity for state intervention in the economy, the Gaullist movement did indeed have affinities with the attitude of the two Napoleons. De Gaulle's use of the referendum, often depicted as Bonapartist, was probably a reaction to the problem of legitimacy during the U-turn of the Algerian war (taking Algeria to independence) than to an affinity with Napoleon III. Likewise the 'Orleanist' strand could be found in de Gaulle's acceptance of the role of business and the market economics of the conservatives recruited into the Fifth Republic's service, such as the economist Jacques Rueff and the small business political figure Antoine Pinay.

De Gaulle does pay homage to the household gods of the conservative sub-cultures but then constructs a synthesis that transcends its original elements, bringing French conservatism into the modern age freed from ancient quarrels and now embracing the Republican idea.[8] Reference has often been made to the religiosity of de Gaulle's family, but he regarded faith as a private business and it did not inform much of his political action. After 1968, when widespread unrest had almost destabilized his regime, de Gaulle turned to ideas incorporated in the papal encyclical *Mater et magister* (1961) notably those of worker participation in industrial decision-making. These themes had not previously been priorities for him. De Gaulle also lacked sympathy with the changes in the 1960s (in personal morality, for example) that were a key element behind the 'events' of 1968. In effect, the brutal shock of the May 1968 events had forced de Gaulle to turn to ideas of social policy that were never fully implemented before his abrupt departure in 1969.

Coming from the milieu of Catholic conservatism as he did, de Gaulle was, notwithstanding, not tempted by the violent and anti-Republican

Action française, although the movement's founder Charles Maurras (1868–1952) admired him. In these traditional Catholic classes the influence of *Action française* was pervasive and it persevered even after its condemnation by the Vatican in 1926. Thus, de Gaulle's condemnation of the party system and his appeal to the nation (a characteristic trope of the far right) made many suspicious of his ambitions, but de Gaulle did not use these terms in a reactionary, 'maurrassien' way and was far more inclusive than *Action française*. De Gaulle was not, however, a Republican in the sense of believing that the National Assembly was the repository of sovereign authority entrusted to it by the French people. In effect, de Gaulle set up a competing legitimacy – the presidency – not recognized in Republican thinking (or in the constitution). De Gaulle's determination to ensure legitimacy through investiture by the Assembly on his return to power in 1958 (by 329–224 votes) was significant in this respect. However, the list of symbols in the cited passage from de Gaulle's *War Memoirs* does not read like a Republican litany. For a Legitimist outlook is clear in de Gaulle's rhetorical denunciation of the Republican elites of parties and in his adoption of a style of monarchical comportment.[9]

Modernizing France

Gaullists regarded themselves as the exemplars of modern and dynamic France (as opposed to the old parties of the previous Republics) and as the artisans of a new beginning.[10] They were, in their own estimation, the harbingers of the scientific, entrepreneurial and far-reaching France that had a cultural '*rayonnement*' like no other European society. De Gaulle's supporter André Malraux (1901–76) claimed that the movement enjoyed broad support throughout French society, comparing it to 'the rush hour crowd on the metro'. This was true, but only to a point; for example, the Gaullist 'crowd' contained few representatives of the idealistic young people who figured so prominently in the events of May 1968.[11]

De Gaulle's conservatism was not a free-market creed. It was more a pragmatism of 'whatever works', designed to develop and bolster the French state wherever this projected French interests. Rémond pointed out that the Gaullist vision was similar to the Bonapartism of the Second Empire in its emphasis on France's position, its determination to pursue the modernization of the country using the leverage of the state and its intent to unify the country. De Gaulle assumed that the purpose of government was to develop the common good and defend the national interest; he dismissed the liberal assumption that these ideas could emerge from a competition between private interests, in which the state merely held the ring. Thus the state, as in Catholic social doctrine, plays a positive role and represents the interests of the national community, rather than abetting the sectional or factional interests which, as de Gaulle saw it, had debilitated previous Republics.

There is a general and national interest, and it does not necessarily coincide with the interests of particular groups and business also had to take its place under the state's purview. One example is the *bouilleurs du cru*, the home-made fruit brandy that was initially distilled by farmers but then passed on as a hereditary right.[12] This right was held by 300,000 or so distillers – few of them farmers – and the inability to act against the 'social scourge' (as it was called) of alcoholism was held against the Fourth Republic. In 1959, the hereditary right was abolished by de Gaulle's government.

France's status

Taken at face value, de Gaulle's attempts to promote France as a major player amid the ideological confrontations and power politics of the Cold War were not plausible. Neither the deployment of French nuclear weapons nor the alliance with West Germany could substitute for support from America (and the North Atlantic Treaty Organization [NATO]) and was misleading. De Gaulle's doctrine on nuclear weapon deployment was incoherent but had the political advantage of high patriotic tone and high visibility.[13] De Gaulle's withdrawal from the NATO military organization in 1966 was designed to show that France – particularly in the Mediterranean theatre – had to be given a substantial role commensurate with its rank. The Gaullist idea that the other European powers, like Chancellor Adenauer's West Germany, could put themselves under French protection verged on the ludicrous.

As set out in the extract, the second aspect of this outlook is the idea of 'Grandeur'. France cannot be France without *Grandeur* – something that is not the same as great power status although the idea of position, respect and authority is encompassed by *Grandeur*. Here the emphasis is on independence and the autonomy of state decision-making. This could be understood to be a swipe at the mediocre ambitions of the previous Republics, and was taken by many to be a commitment to Empire; but in de Gaulle's lexicon it meant that France had to take its place as one of the Great Powers and to be taken seriously. Thus, de Gaulle's famous and flamboyant vetoes of the United Kingdom's application to join the European Economic Community (EEC) (1963 and 1967) and his controversial speech in Quebec in July 1967 were used to project French influence within and beyond Europe.[14]

De Gaulle's Europe

Despite his vetoes of UK membership of the EEC (at least in part on the pretext that the country was insufficiently 'Communitaire') de Gaulle's own attitude to European integration was not wholly dissimilar to the views of British 'Eurosceptics', in the 1960s and later. His position was based on the Common Market's potential to restrict states' freedom of action. This, of course, neglected the way that the EEC, established under the Fourth Republic, promoted and amplified the position of France itself. In the event, and with calculation, the French position in Europe was not dismantled by de Gaulle, and Europe was used to advance French interests, notably in agriculture.[15]

De Gaulle's idea of an intergovernmental Europe of nation states was close to the United Kingdom's and far from the project of the original founders, including his countryman Jean Monnet (1888–1979).[16] De Gaulle's writings depict Europe as a continent in which the old states performed a stately minuet in an eighteenth-century balance of power. This Europe no longer existed and was obviously at odds with the ideological divisions of Europe into two blocs in east and west, with the east controlled by the USSR. Moreover, de Gaulle's Europe would be under French rather than American leadership. De Gaulle's dismissal of the United Kingdom as an American Trojan Horse failed to recognize that the enemy was already inside the walls: West Germany would not exchange the Atlantic partnership for a French-led community. De Gaulle's construction of a Franco-German special relationship built on European foundations was limited by *realpolitik* which underlined the dominance of the United States in European affairs.

De Gaulle's notion of French independence ran against the impediments of international institutions and that included the United Nations. However, his vision was also a way of asserting a French individuality and providing cover for an eccentric path in foreign relations that accomplished the aim of reviving France's position as a power that had to be reckoned with, even if de Gaulle himself had to accept that it was not a 'super-power' like the United States and the USSR. By the same token, de Gaulle believed that France enjoyed a special concord with the USSR. Unrealistic as it was, de Gaulle's determined re-establishment of France as a major actor on the European stage was successful in its short-term purpose of maintaining national pride after the repeated humiliations of the 1940s and 1950s, and left a more lasting legacy in French foreign policy. This emphasis on French culture and policy, it should be remembered, came at a time when the Communist Party was strong and when the centrists of the Fourth Republic took European integration as their issue. Communists polled about 20% of the vote in this period and proclaimed their attachment to the Soviet Union, the workers' fatherland, and their ideological influence was enormous. Socialists and other centre parties were internationalist in outlook and at this time were proud of their role in promoting European institutions.

Although de Gaulle's assumption that the European Cold War division would be effaced as the old nationalisms reasserted themselves was not dropped, the invasion of Czechoslovakia by the Warsaw Pact Armies in 1968 contradicted his viewpoint. Soviet armed intervention to replace the fleeting liberalism of the 'Prague Spring' with a compliant and repressive regime showed that it was unrealistic in the short term. In particular, de Gaulle's assumption that the end of the Cold War would lead to a Europe in which France was the preponderant power took no account of how France could handle a united Germany which would be inevitably preponderant on the continent. De Gaulle's mid-1960s strategy of undermining the US dollar with the intent of creating a new gold standard was also unrealistic but, perhaps, something of an irritation in the monetary system then in operation.

De Gaulle was of the generation and background that regarded the Empire and imperial mission as part and parcel of French international politics. Yet it fell to him to complete decolonization, started in the Fourth Republic, and to determine the independence of Algeria – ending the most difficult and longest of French colonial wars. Although he knew that the opponents of Algerian independence would never forgive him, de Gaulle covered France's retreat by adopting the language of liberation, now posing as the champion of the developing new nations. Again, on an objective view this was highly improbable, given France's recent history and its inability to offer tangible support to liberation movements. Yet his tactics were based on a shrewd calculation of attitudes in France, and arguably were crucial in bringing his country through the crisis.

It may have been helpful to de Gaulle that the nuclear *force de frappe* provided another role for the French forces and a boost to French status.[17] Developed under the Fourth Republic, but accelerated considerably by de Gaulle, the French nuclear programme marked a concerted attempt to make up for lost ground in this crucial race for national *Grandeur*. Since the country had placed itself outside NATO's nuclear umbrella, the weapons were undeniably French; but at the time, their delivery depended on an aircraft strike force that was of doubtful value compared to the superpower arsenals of ballistic missiles.[18] De Gaulle's nuclear doctrine, developed to justify this weaponry, became part of the national consensus despite its obvious limitations as military strategy.

Conservative leadership

Gaullism is, thus, a form of forceful political leadership and as such marks a recognition of de Gaulle's status and authority. De Gaulle's ideas lack originality when their various elements are judged in isolation, but in combination they represent a distinctive form of conservatism. In his memoirs, de Gaulle refers to the 'ferments of dispersion' inherent in the nature of the French as a people but thanks to his ideas as well as his personal charisma he was able to project the French state as a binding force at a time when it was faced by a variety of disruptive forces.

De Gaulle had made clear his view that authoritative political leadership had to be provided in a Republican era but without the trappings of dictatorship that disfigured the century. He was reprising the frequent accusation by the right and left, that the Republic's leadership was inadequate and that the emergence of the much-needed visionary leader was impeded by its introspective parliamentary elite in the Assembly. But the intention of Gaullism was not to sweep away parliamentary institutions; it was to provide leadership to them, supported by the French people.[19] De Gaulle stated that '*la grandeur d'un people ne procède que de ce peuple*'. Yet in de Gaulle's view, the people was represented by their leader: They were in harmony. De Gaulle's belief was that he could unite a majority of the French public behind him. His conviction proved well founded in the late 1940s with the RPF movement and then in the Fifth Republic (until the repudiation of his referendum in 1969 when he drew the obvious conclusion and retired). Thus, de Gaulle spoke, in his estimation, not as a politician but as an authentic voice of the country itself.

Conclusion

Rather than accepting the 'conservative' label, Gaullists preferred to see themselves as transcending divisions of left and right and regarded themselves as the real progressives in France. This outlook was symbolized by the Gaullist deputies who, when they won the general elections in 1962, occupied the Assembly arc from left to right and forced the old parties to the back benches. But Gaullism does take its place as a conservative movement through its focus on the nation and its preoccupation with stability at a time of significant geopolitical change. After the humiliation of the French Army in the Second World War, followed quickly by capitulation in Vietnam after the defeat at Dien Bien Phu and the Algerian imbroglio, it was essential for someone to uphold the integrity of the nation as well as salvaging something of the country's international status. It is to de Gaulle's credit as a consummate politician that at a time of crisis he was able to establish the leading role of the French presidency, and to inspire a political movement which continued to cherish his example, of a style of governance and a general attitude to fast-changing events at home and abroad, which continued to attract significant support decades after his death.

CHAPTER FIFTEEN

Ronald Reagan

Donald Critchlow

First inaugural speech, 20 January 1981

In this present crisis, government is not the solution to our problem; government is the problem. From time to time we've been tempted to believe that society has become too complex to be managed by self-rule, that government by an elite group is superior to government for, by, and of the people. Well, if no one among us is capable of governing himself, then who among us has the capacity to govern someone else? All of us together, in and out of government, must bear the burden. The solutions we seek must be equitable, with no one group singled out to pay a higher price ...

We are a nation that has a government – not the other way around. And this makes us special among the nations of the Earth. Our government has no power except that granted it by the people. It is time to check and reverse the growth of government, which shows signs of having grown beyond the consent of the governed.

It is my intention to curb the size and influence of the Federal establishment and to demand recognition of the distinction between the powers granted to the Federal Government and those reserved to the States or to the people. All of us need to be reminded that the Federal Government did not create the States; the States created the Federal Government.

Now, so there will be no misunderstanding, it's not my intention to do away with government. It is rather to make it work – work with us, not over us; to stand by our side, not ride on our back. Government can and must provide opportunity, not smother it; foster productivity, not stifle it.

If we look to the answer as to why for so many years we achieved so much, prospered as no other people on Earth, it was because here in this land we unleashed the energy and individual genius of man to a greater extent than has ever been done before. Freedom and the dignity of the individual have been more available and assured here than in any other place on Earth. The price for this freedom at times has been high, but we have never been unwilling to pay that price.

It is no coincidence that our present troubles parallel and are proportionate to the intervention and intrusion in our lives that result from unnecessary and excessive growth of government. It is time for us to realize that we're too great a nation to limit ourselves to small dreams. We're not, as some would have us believe, doomed to an inevitable decline . . .

We have every right to dream heroic dreams. Those who say that we're in a time when there are not heroes, they just don't know where to look ... Now, I have used the words 'they' and 'their' in speaking of these heroes. I could say 'you' and 'your', because I'm addressing the heroes of whom I speak – you, the citizens of this blessed land. Your dreams, your hopes, your goals are going to be the dreams, the hopes, and the goals of this administration, so help me God.[1]

Ronald Reagan's inaugural address on 20 January 1981 projected his eloquence and ability to speak to the hopes and dreams of average Americans, following a decade of American economic turmoil, three failed presidencies and apparent decline as a world power. Reagan's greatest strength was displayed on the public podium. He captured the deep patriotism of average Americans, spoke in words simple to understand but eloquent in composition and projected their firm belief that their hopes for themselves, their families and the nation would be realized.

Reagan's speech reflected the fears and the aspiration of Americans in 1981. Reagan achieved a landslide victory in the 1980 election against incumbent President Jimmy Carter. Carter's presidency had been caught in the riptides of history, runaway inflation and rising unemployment, an adventurist Soviet Union taking advantage of American-perceived loss of power and finally rising Islamic militancy seen in the Iranian Revolution in 1979. Reagan won the Republican nomination after fighting off primary challenges by George H. W. Bush and other candidates. During the primaries, Reagan made plenty of gaffes and often got his facts wrong, and at times seemed insecure and indecisive. Yet his message for scaling back government, increasing defense spending and restoring America compensated for any weakness on the campaign trail.

In nominating Reagan, the Republican Party confirmed its shift to the right that had begun with Barry Goldwater's nomination in 1964. Reagan's selection of George H. W. Bush, a moderate, as his running mate, signaled to party leaders and the public that he was not a right-wing loon.

The Reagan–Bush campaign knew that if the election turned into a replay of 1976, Reagan would lose. Carter's narrow victory over incumbent

President Gerald Ford was largely due to Carter's ability to win Southern states. If Reagan was going to defeat Carter, Republicans needed to carry the South. In addition, Reagan needed to persuade blue-collar workers that he was not an extremist out to eliminate every federal entitlement program. In his nominating speech for Reagan at the Republican National Convention, Senator Paul Laxalt (R-Nevada) emphasized Reagan's record as Governor of California of increasing benefits for the truly needy, increasing funding for education, protecting the environment and initiating welfare reform.

The Reagan campaign understood as well that if they were to win the White House, they needed to win over evangelical Protestant Christian voters who had gone for Carter in 1976. As a result, during the campaign, Reagan hammered on his support for religious liberty and anti-abortion, and his belief in the traditional family. Reagan performed well in debates and gave enough assurance to the public that he could be trusted in a nuclear world. Even with news networks reporting daily on the Iranian crisis when radical Islamist revolutionaries took American embassy workers hostage, the Carter campaign continued to believe until the final few days that they were going to win the election. Carter and his team underestimated Reagan, as so many others had done in the past.

Still, few predicted Reagan's landslide victory on the election night, in which he won 489 electoral votes to Carter's 49, taking 44 states. Reagan carried the South by five percentage points, the Midwest by as much as ten points in some states and the West by nearly 20 points. Blue-collar workers swung heavily to Reagan.

Reagan won the election as an avowed conservative. His campaign rhetoric expressed his conservative principles, and was often heated, at times alarming those on the left. In office he stuck to his core principles of lower taxes, reducing social spending and strengthening national defense. His cabinet choices were mostly conservatives who aligned with his principles.

Much has been made of Reagan the rhetorician. Critics caricatured him as an actor just mouthing words written for him by behind-the-scene powerful interests – wealthy corporate interests – who sought to beguile American voters with social issues, in order to get what they really wanted: tax cuts for themselves. Reagan's opponents labeled him the 'Teflon President', who easily deflected dirt thrown at him by his critics.

No doubt Reagan was a master at public speaking. Reagan had honed his skills in speaking to average Americans as a spokesperson for General Electric in the 1950s, espousing the virtues of capitalism – a featured speaker at anti-communist rallies and Republican events and a successful politician who was elected governor of the most populous state, California. Reagan's affable personality came across on the stage. His rhetoric could be heated, and to his critics, was often over the top. His delivery, though, was natural, his voice calm, and inspiring without being condescending.

The underlying strength of Reagan as a speaker and a politician rested on his core principles, articulated in his First Inaugural Address. He believed as a conservative that ultimately freedom depended upon citizens, acting as individuals, to better themselves, their families and their communities through voluntary action. This assumption is made clear in the speech, when Reagan declares,

> If we look to the answer as to why for so many years we achieved so much, prospered as no other people on Earth, it was because here in this land we unleashed the energy and individual genius of man to a greater extent than has ever been done before. Freedom and the dignity of the individual have been more available and assured here than in any other place on Earth.

His following sentence captures another core principle held by Reagan, that freedom often comes at a cost: 'The price for this freedom at times has been high, but we have never been unwilling to pay that price.'

These two principles, individual voluntary action and the defense of freedom, determined Reagan's view of government. In his inaugural address, he declares that

> Government is not the solution to our problem; government is the problem. From time to time we've been tempted to believe that society has become too complex to be managed by self-rule, that government by an elite group is superior to government for, by, and of the people. Well, if no one among us is capable of governing himself, then who among us has the capacity to govern someone else?

Reagan expressed a confidence in individuals to decide best what is best for themselves. Government, he declares, is not the solution to the nation's problems. Indeed, government intrusion has caused many of the nation's problems. As a consequence, he calls in his speech for downsizing the government through economic deregulation and returning more power to the states. State governments, he implies, should be laboratories of experiment. Reagan made clear that he was not a libertarian purist who believed that any government involvement in the economy or social welfare was evil. Indeed, as president, he undertook Social Security reform, which raised individual and employment contributions and extended the age requirements for receiving benefits. Under his administration, large block grants for welfare, specifically Aid to Families with Dependent Children, were made to the states. An economic recession early in his first term forced him to agree to raise corporate taxes on two occasions, but he held steadfast to individual income tax reductions. In his second term, he worked with Democrats to simplify the tax system.

He believed that government's primary responsibility was to maintain national security. This entailed a strong, if not superior, military. Throughout the decade of the 1970s and in his presidential campaigns in

1976 and 1980, he assailed Democrats for cutting back on defense spending. In his bid for the Republican nomination in 1976, he attacked incumbent President Gerald Ford for selling out American interests and potentially weakening national defense by turning over the Panama Canal Zone to Panama, ruled by anti-American dictators. He joined defense hawks, including Democrats such as Senator Henry Jackson (D-Washington) and Paul Nitze, in opposition to the Strategic Arms Limitation Treaty II. Following the Soviet invasion of Afghanistan in 1979, President Carter withdrew the treaty from Senate consideration.

Reagan's core ideological principles about strengthening American defense and ensuring American nuclear superiority were evident in his administration's subsequent foreign policy. As president, Reagan pursued a huge military build-up. His order to install medium-range missiles in Europe sparked massive international demonstrations calling for a unilateral nuclear freeze. Reagan's denunciation of the Soviet Union as an 'evil empire' raised concerns among his critics that he was placing the world on the edge of a nuclear war. The culmination of his foreign policy came in his second term with the signing of a major and verifiable arms control reduction treaty with the Soviet Union. Reagan's foreign policy set the stage for the end of the Cold War that came in George H. W. Bush's administration.

What is most evident in Reagan's inaugural address and his subsequent administration was his *principled pragmatism*, the capacity to maintain core principles, while achieving political and legislative success without betraying these principles. Reagan's belief that people are best deciding for themselves what is best for themselves entailed minimal government interference in their lives. He held essential to the preservation of a constitutional, representative republic a financially healthy government and a strong, well-prepared national defense to protect the nation. He sought, therefore, lower individual taxes to allow average Americans more freedom to spend their money where they wanted, and a strong military to protect the nation. These were his core principles.

On other matters he proved to be a compromiser. He understood that successful legislation was an act of compromise. Most often in legislation, neither side got fully want they wanted. Sometimes, a principled politician might agree to a legislative bill that was not fully satisfactory, but such a bill might accomplish some of what was being sought and might set the stage for more important bills to come. Reagan's principled pragmatism was evidenced in his political campaigns. When staff and donors brought to him what appeared to be irreconcilable differences, Reagan adroitly found a middle ground that satisfied both sides. He understood that the campaign's purpose was to win office and achieve principled goals.

Reagan's ability to seek legislative compromise had been evident during his governorship when he worked with Democrats to achieve model welfare reform. During his California governor's race against incumbent Pat Brown in 1966, Reagan presented himself as 'citizen-politician' who could bring common sense to government. His tone was moderate, but his message was solidly conservative.[2]

After his landslide election victory, he stepped into the governor's office without a great understanding of government. Reagan's faith, as expressed in Goldwater's campaign speech in 1964, 'A Time for Choosing,' that 'the truth is there are simple answers – they're just not easy ones', did not provide a policy agenda or an understanding of the complexities of governing. Most on his 1966 campaign staff did not know much about state government and the legislative process.

The first steps in governing proved difficult for Reagan and his staff. They could not even find a suitable budget director, and when Caspar Weinberger, an experienced California legislator, was proposed, he was shot down by his aide Robert Tuttle because Weinberger was seen as a liberal Republican who had supported Nelson Rockefeller in the California presidential primary in 1964. Reagan and his staff, however, proved to be quick learners. Reagan deferred to his experts, but at executive meetings he zeroed in on the critical issues, kept to his core principles, and showed he was a masterful negotiator. Lou Cannon, who watched the administration first hand, concluded that 'Reagan was simultaneously conservative and pragmatic.'[3] Reagan clung to his principles without allowing them to undermine his governance.

Reagan developed a working relationship with the legislature, especially the upper house. He did not try to pretend he was 'one of the boys'. Instead, he developed a strong legislative affairs office – a pattern followed when he became president. Left with a huge state budget deficit by the Brown administration, Reagan agreed to the largest tax hike in state history – 'a breathtaking display of pragmatism', as Cannon put it.[4] In negotiations with Democratic Assembly Speaker Jesse Unruh, Reagan lost on many issues, but took what he could get. After signing the radical tax legislation, Reagan might have been in deep political trouble with voters. After all, he ran on a campaign to lower taxes and shrink government. He deflected the issue by accusing the previous administration of having left the state with a major deficit. Over the next seven years, the California state economy prospered and his administration experienced budget surpluses.

For most of his two terms in office, Reagan faced a Democratic-controlled legislature. One consequence was that he found himself having to sign legislation he did not necessarily agree with, including budget cuts in mental health and an extremely liberal abortion bill. Reagan wanted to veto the abortion bill, but Republican legislators had voted for the bill, and he did not leave them out on a political limb. His greatest accomplishment, however, came in his second term with welfare reform. Reagan won re-election in 1970 against Democratic challenger Jesse Unruh. During the re-election campaign, Reagan promised to reform the welfare system. Winning a decisive second term, Reagan made this a high priority.

Reagan opposed Nixon's proposed Family Assistant Plan, which would have provided, in effect, a guaranteed income for the poor. In a television debate, Reagan declared, 'I believe that the government is supposed to promote the general welfare. I don't believe it's supposed to provide it.'[5] Instead, working with Assembly Speaker Bob Moretti, an ultra-liberal from Northern California, Reagan and his team entered into tough negotiations to undertake welfare reform. Negotiations often lasted from morning through night to craft what became at the time a model for welfare reform. The California Welfare Reform raised benefits, decreased eligibility and established a demonstration work program. Within three years, welfare rolls had dropped by nearly 300,000 people.

Reagan carried into the presidency his legislative experience as a governor. He stood firmly on set principles, while remaining pragmatic as to what could be accomplished. As president, Reagan held that it was necessary to compromise to get 75 or 80 per cent of his program, and that this was worth the compromise. Reagan was willing to make legislative compromises, but not in relation to core principles of individual tax cuts and a strong national defense.

The Reagan presidency, while being called the Reagan Revolution by his supporters, came with costs. As president, he did not succeed in every initiative. The belief that tax cuts would spark enough economic growth to enhance revenues proved only partially true. Economic growth did create more revenue, but not enough to compensate for the costs of defense spending. He failed to achieve his campaign promise to overturn *Roe v. Wade,* or his pledge to disband the Department of Education.[6] Although Reagan cut staffing of regulatory agencies in the Consumer Protection Safety Commission, the Occupational Safety and Health Administration and the Environmental Protection Agency, the regulatory state remained intact. In 1982, a national recession forced him to agree to an increase in the corporate tax rate, but this had been preceded the previous year by the largest tax cut in American history. In implementing Social Security reform, Reagan agreed to increased payroll taxes and extending age requirements for receiving benefits. The administration's anti-communist opposition to the pro-Soviet Sandinista regime in Nicaragua created an environment for what became known as the Iran-Contra scandal. As a result, Reagan's two terms as president were not without flaws, mishaps and policy errors that had long-term consequences.

These perceived failures to fulfill his campaign promises have led to a sizeable literature that the Reagan Revolution failed.[7] Even his apparent success in foreign policy brought heavy criticism from later scholars. The collapse of the Soviet Union, Reagan's liberal critics argue, would have occurred without Reagan because of the inherent weakness of the Soviet Union. Conservative defenders, politicians and journalists tend to emphasize Reagan's ideological purity. Yet, whatever the specific record of the Reagan administration, he achieved much of what he promised in his inaugural address.

His greatest success came in reaching accommodation with the Soviet Union by negotiating a verifiable arms control treaty. He set the stage for ending the Cold War, which occurred shortly after he left office. He tempered ideological principle, while maintaining core conservative values about the nature of government, the value of a free market in economic development and asserting that freedom is always one generation removed from extinction. He distrusted centralized government without calling for its complete dismantling.

Reagan's immediate legacy after leaving office was having achieved tax simplification, lower income rates for average Americans, economic deregulation and arms control. He did not achieve everything he promised. The 'iron-triangle' of congressional committees, federal bureaucrats and interest groups endured, a fact he lamented on 14 December 1988, shortly before he was to leave the White House.[8] He had failed to overturn or reform abortion expressed in the *Roe v. Wade* case of 1973. Many of his appointments to the Supreme Court and lower federal courts failed to live up to conservative expectations.

Reagan's successes and his ability to communicate conservative ideas to the larger public made him into an icon of the Republican Party, which became the party of Lincoln and Reagan. His greatest legacy, however, has tended to be overlooked by both admirers and critics: his *principled pragmatism*. Sixty years later, with a highly polarized electorate and many party leaders given more to maintaining ideological principle than the art of politics, Reagan's capacity to compromise, while maintaining core principles, should be recalled. He articulated optimism without seeking perfection in government or humankind. He expressed a deep faith in the American Dream, and he understood that dreams can become reality when acted upon through *realpolitik*.

CHAPTER SIXTEEN

Margaret Thatcher (1925–2013)

Kieron O'Hara

I think we've been through a period where too many people have been given to understand that if they have a problem, it's the government's job to cope with it. 'I have a problem, I'll get a grant.' 'I'm homeless, the government must house me.' They're casting their problems on society. And you know, there's no such thing as society. There are individual men and women, there are families. And no government can do anything except through people, and people must look after themselves first. It's our duty to look after ourselves and then, also, to look after our neighbours. People have got the entitlements too much in mind, without the obligations. There's no such thing as entitlement, unless someone has first met an obligation.[1]

Margaret Thatcher is unique in this volume in that her most famous venture into philosophy appeared in an outlet better known for recipes, celebrity gossip and agony columns. The above excerpt, from an interview she gave to the lifestyle magazine *Woman's Own* in October 1987, became the focus of considerable ridicule and outrage.

The medium of a magazine interview was characteristic of a politician who, though not an original theoretician, was a notable communicator – as her political opponent Tony Benn suggested, a great teacher[2] – whose political success rested upon appealing to elements of the electorate whom other members of her party had never come close to reaching. But it took a long time for the Conservative Party to live down this particular interview. Thatcher herself muttered that her meaning had been 'distorted beyond recognition',[3] into a supposed celebration of hard-hearted Tory devil-take-the-hindmost individualism. Eventually, while campaigning for the Conservative leadership in 2005, David Cameron settled on the argument that 'We know we have a shared responsibility, that we're all in this together, that there is such a thing as society; it's just not the same thing as the state,'[4] and promoted his idea of the 'big society' in order to put the nagging issue to bed.

Thatcher's status is problematic. She self-identified as conservative, but was equally proud of her radicalism. *The Downing Street Years*, her most comprehensive presentation of her own ideas,[5] presents an energetic and iconoclastic figure who was also reasonably candid about the practical checks on her powers, and the consequent need to pick her fights judiciously.[6] It is partisan, written shortly after her defenestration as prime minister in November 1990, when memories of that bitter time were still strong. Although it is a vital source, it is hardly a neutral account of the evolution of her thinking, especially in the earlier period of her premiership.

This chapter explores three questions. First, what is the nature of Thatcher's political philosophy, and in particular the uncompromising statement that 'there is no such thing as society'? Second, can we judge whether her policies in office were consistent with a tenable understanding of conservatism? Third, can we trace some of the antecedents of her thinking, and place her, tentatively at least, within a tradition?

Thatcher's journey

Nothing in Margaret Thatcher's career prior to 1974 suggested an underlying determination to launch an aggressive challenge against her party's establishment and accepted parameters of the politically possible. She served loyally in Edward Heath's cabinet (1970–74), and her most prominent ideological statement before then, her Conservative Party Centre (CPC) lecture of 1968, was not outspokenly radical. Indeed, Thatcher reproached herself later for not developing her pre-existing ideas into a coherent framework.[7] Some[8] have found her claim to have been a consistent Hayekian[9] somewhat unconvincing, but many of the themes prominent in her later thinking, such as the importance of citizens' independence of government, and the link between hard work and higher income, were present in her CPC lecture.[10]

A not inaccurate caricature of Conservative Party history from 1945 to 1975 is that of an ongoing attempt to recover from the psychological blow of its landslide electoral defeat in 1945. Broadly speaking, there were two classes of response. The 'orthodox' approach, amply represented in the senior ranks of the party, accepted at least part of the argument for planning, welfare and economic controls, and claimed to be better able to manage these in government than the Labour Party. The resulting consensus may have been overplayed by commentators, but is broadly persuasive. Electorally, the strategy was reasonably successful, and produced seventeen years of Tory government out of thirty.

Many Conservative Party members, however, resented dancing to the other party's tune. The second response was therefore resistance, often based on the free-market arguments of F. A. Hayek's *The Road to Serfdom* (1944). The mutual consistency of markets and conservatism seemed clear in two respects. First, change via the decisions of individuals in a free market appeared 'organic' in a way that change imposed from Whitehall did not; and second, a free market would increase personal responsibility and minimize free riding on the welfare state, by exposing individuals to the consequences of their actions. The leading proponent of this view, Enoch Powell, caused a mixture of puzzlement and fear among his colleagues on the Conservative front bench, from which he was sacked in 1968 after expressing his forthright views on immigration.[11]

The party leader after 1965, Edward Heath, tried to establish a position in opposition which was distinct from both the 'consensus' and the views of Hayek. In government, however, he reversed direction in the face of growing unemployment, adopting an inflationary Keynesian economic policy instead. After its ignominious failure and the fall of Heath's government in February 1974, the ex-minister Sir Keith Joseph began to propound his view that conservatism had been neglected by the Conservative Party.[12] After a further Conservative defeat in October 1974, Joseph looked set to challenge Heath for the leadership; his ally Thatcher stepped into his shoes when he decided not to run.

Thatcher and Conservative ideology

As Conservative leader, Thatcher took on board the untested theory of monetarism, to the anger of anti-theoretic Conservatives.[13] Thatcher herself argued that she applied the theory judiciously,[14] and its use as an organizing principle for the reforms she wished to introduce, particularly in public spending,[15] does not in itself rule her out as a conservative. She despised the political skill of compromise.[16] Nevertheless, there is nothing necessarily conservative about compromise, and nothing necessarily compromising about conservatism.

Thatcher (in her memoirs) more or less conflates conservatism and the radical free-market ideas of Hayek.[17] As has been argued by conservatives since Burke, conservatism does not rule out change, even radical change. The point of conservatism is to raise the barriers to change, and to put the burden of proof of social value onto the innovator.[18] This entails that a conservative can support radical policies when the status quo is (by some relevant measure) unsatisfactory, because the risk of harm from the innovation is outweighed by the risks of stasis. Britain in the 1970s was widely perceived as an economic and social basket case;[19] in Thatcher's words, 'Britain in 1979 was a nation that had had the stuffing knocked out of it.' 'Everything we wished to do [in 1979] had to fit into the overall strategy of reversing Britain's economic decline [while] however difficult the road might be … we intended to achieve a fundamental change of direction', even if this 'would not be possible without some measure of discord'.[20]

One relevant metric was the nation's international reputation. Even the Falklands War was fought 'to defend our honour as a nation',[21] and victory was celebrated as showing that 'We have ceased to be a nation in retreat.' National character was a real aspect of personality, so 'Reversing our economic decline was one part of the task of restoring Britain's reputation; demonstrating that we were not the sort of people to bow before dictators was another.' Her subsequent criticism of the European Union (EU) was based on the worry that 'British democracy, parliamentary sovereignty, the common law, our traditional sense of fairness, our ability to run our affairs in our own way [would] be subordinated to the demands of a remote European bureaucracy, resting on very different traditions'. She was concerned, like Burke, that 'our country ought to be lovely',[22] and sounded another Burkean note in her party's 1983 election manifesto, invoking 'a great chain of people stretching back into the past and forwards into the future … linked by a common belief in freedom, and in Britain's greatness. All are aware of their own responsibility to contribute to both'.[23] Note how Thatcher went beyond even Burke's active notion of a partnership or contract among the living, the dead and the yet to be born, by emphasizing the particular duties that members of the chain must undertake.

Thatcher's practice

Thatcher's abiding aim was to change the relationship between the individual and the state, focusing on 'the extension of choice, the dispersal of power and the encouragement of responsibility'. The sale of council houses, for example, created a sudden increase in property ownership (and therefore, on conservative thinking, in the number of people with a stronger interest in stability), while reducing the influence of the state, or local councils, over the population.[24]

Michael Oakeshott argued that innovation should be a means to correct an existing problem, not to displace theoretical opportunity costs or implement a vision of perfection.[25] From this point of view, Thatcher's first term of office had conservative aspects, dealing with a range of identified problems from militant trade unionism to stifling tax rates.[26] Oakeshott's distinction, however, is not always straightforward to make out in practice. Thatcher argued that Britain's problem was, at least in part, a 'centralizing, managerial, bureaucratic, interventionist style of government' associated with the post-war consensus. Intervention covered a wide range of contingencies, and governments would even 'run advertising campaigns to persuade people of the virtues of dependence' on the ground that a 'disinterested civil service, with access to the best and latest information, was better able to foresee economic eventualities and to propose responses to them than were the blind forces of the so-called "free market".' Though the Conservative Party opposed this doctrine in principle, its governments 'never tried seriously to reverse it'.[27] She was determined not to flinch from the challenge.

Thatcher thought that civil associations were undermined by the state. For instance, she strongly rejected the common claim that the urban riots of 1981 were an indication that economic policy was causing social breakdown. She insisted that the deprivation and squalor of the troubled estates would have galvanized communities to clear up the mess if they weren't lacking both respect for the law and 'a sense of pride and personal responsibility – something that the state can easily remove but almost never give back'. The well-being of democracy depended on 'limitation of the powers of government, a market economy, private property – and the sense of personal responsibility without which no such system could be sustained'.[28]

Trade union reform could also be cast as a removal of a problem in Oakeshott's sense. As Thatcher put it, 'trade union immunities had combined with nationalized monopolies to give huge power to the trade unions in these industries'. Furthermore, she believed, not irrationally, that some trade unionists were trying to overthrow her government. Context was all; unions were not necessarily bad. For example, they were important in Poland because the Poles did not have free elections or other means of expressing themselves.[29]

Her union reforms often (though not always) involved changes to civil law, not criminal law, so that holding unions to account for the consequences of their actions would be left to companies or dissatisfied trade unionists, rather than a prescriptive government. Government's job was merely 'to establish a framework of stability – whether constitutional stability, the rule of law, or the economic stability produced by sound money – within which individual families and businesses were free to pursue their own dreams and ambitions'.[30] In the end, though, Thatcher's belief that unions caused unemployment by raising the price of labour in the absence of productivity improvements resulted in an acceleration of the reforms.

In her first term, the problems Thatcher addressed had been widely accepted as pressing priorities, but as her confidence grew and divisions within the ranks of the opposition made her position seem impregnable, her judgements grew more personal and opportunistic, as with privatization of state-owned industries.[31] The 1986 'Big Bang', the deregulation of the City of London, was a naked attempt to reduce opportunity costs – hardly the 'natural corollary to the earlier abolition of exchange controls' presented by Cannadine.[32] Her resolutely non-interventionist approach to economics contrasted sharply with her later forays into social policy, which betrayed her desire to 'strengthen ... the traditional virtues'. In Oakeshottian terms, this was merely a variant of the left-wing characterization of the state as an 'enterprise association'. In education, she abandoned her 'healthy distrust of the state using central control of the syllabus as a means of propaganda', and developed a national curriculum to counter the influence of 'left-wing local authorities, teachers and pressure groups', though in the end this merely opened new interventionist opportunities for the Department for Education and Science. She was reluctant to see fundamental changes in the National Health Service (NHS) because it 'delivered a high quality of care ... at a reasonably modest unit cost', but favoured a review because it was a 'bottomless money pit'. Yet even there, she became worried because, 'under Treasury pressure' the government was 'moving away from, rather than towards, radical reforms'.[33]

A possible source?

Following the defeat of the Conservatives in February 1974, Thatcher found Joseph's new intellectual position congenial. This combined a concern with the government's fiscal rectitude (expressed in her early years of office in the theory of monetarism, although that was ultimately abandoned, on the grounds that money was too difficult to measure[34]), with emphasis on (i) the importance of an individual's own endeavour within a framework of free enterprise to shore up both that individual's self-respect and welfare, and wider prosperity, and (ii) the concomitant dangers of socialism and welfarism undermining that framework and gradually chipping away at self-reliance. Yet Thatcher did not emulate Joseph's genuine agonizing about the problems of those who are not equipped, perhaps because of poor education, poverty, deprivation or addiction, to use their freedom constructively within a free market.[35] In the words of Thatcher's biographer, 'Joseph was the intellectual driving force of Thatcherism, but he was also, by character, a Hamlet.'[36] In contrast, Thatcher was more likely to bring Coriolanus to mind.

Was Thatcher's individualism so complete that social aggregations greater than the family were irrelevant to her, as a variety of critics have alleged on the basis of the *Woman's Own* interview? One potential, and neglected, source of her thinking that may also serve as a point of comparison is Angus Maude's philosophical tract *The Common Problem*.

Maude was, like his friend Enoch Powell, a Conservative dissenter from the post-war consensus; and, like Powell, he was sacked from Edward Heath's Shadow Cabinet. He worked with Thatcher during and after her leadership campaign, and was rewarded with a place in her first cabinet. His philosophy of self-reliance and individualism was somewhat romantic and, in its time, *sui generis*.[37] Much of his argument derives from an analysis on the topic of 'society', which he conceived to be a statistical abstraction of no relevance. He deplores, in Tocquevillian terms, the dissolving of Burke's 'little platoons' by larger, less heterogeneous and more predictable statistical abstractions, and the severing of connections with the past.[38] 'It is *not* "society" that provides social security, but State administrators dispensing the taxpayers' money. There is *not* a "social conscience" – only individuals laboriously seeking to persuade an apathetic (but vaguely benevolent) majority of the need for reforms. There are no "social needs" – only people in trouble, who need to be thought of and helped as people'.[39]

Maude argued that, in a world where statistical patterns of mass behaviour have become accepted as norms,

> The bewildered individual, seeking lost authority, certainty and standards, is reduced to social conformism. It is a kind of 'back to the womb' movement, or at the least a demand not to grow out of the childhood state of security without responsibility. And 'society' is expected to provide the security. Here we have the demand for 'social security', which means that 'society' must increasingly take over the moral and financial responsibilities of individuals and families. But 'society', of course, cannot do this, for it does not exist.[40]

There may or may not be a causal connection between Maude's work and Thatcher's philosophy. Thatcher paid tribute to Maude's 'sound views' in her memoirs,[41] but their personal connection seems to have ended when, aged 69, Maude resigned from her cabinet. *The Common Problem* (unlike *Change is Our Ally*, a CPC pamphlet Maude co-edited with Enoch Powell in 1954) is mentioned neither in her memoirs nor in any of the major biographies.

Yet the parallels are clear, and also help us diagnose the political problem of Thatcher's provocative phrases. Unlike Maude, she mentions no intermediate units between families and societies. But her positive point, that people are better off in all senses if they take control of their own environments, follows him. She also made much, in the *Woman's Own* interview and elsewhere, of the importance of behavioural and moral standards, another major theme of Maude's.[42]

We noted earlier that Thatcher's organic vision of a 'great chain' stretching backwards and forwards in time emphasized the responsibilities of individuals to forge the links themselves. Like Maude, Thatcher rejected a vision of society as a set of abstract forces with the cumulative capability of becoming an agent in its own right, taking over responsibility for individuals' agency, housing them, clearing up their neighbourhoods and keeping them secure. And with Maude too, she argued that the state agencies which offer to take on this role are not merely harmless props which ameliorate some of the drudgery of existence and help citizens feel more secure, at the (minor?) cost of infantilizing them. Taking responsibility for one's own duties is essential not only for sustaining one's identity as a free, autonomous individual, but also in sustaining the social relationships that underpin a vigorous and healthy democracy.[43]

Thatcher's legacy

Among his many idiosyncratic views, Maude believed that 'the acquisitive wealthy may be a greater menace to the private property of others, and more careless of its rights, than the State itself'.[44] Thatcher, by contrast, was extremely relaxed on this subject. In the *Woman's Own* interview, she remarked that working for money

> is the great driving engine, the driving force of life. There is nothing wrong with having a lot more money ... . It is not the fact of having money. It is whether it becomes the sole or only thing in your life and you want money because it is money. The exercise of the spirit and the inspiration is what you do with that money. There is nothing wrong in wanting more.[45]

Yet, despite Thatcher's moral injunctions, people did not seem to use their freedom as prudently as they might. Newly liberated from controls on spending and borrowing, individuals still consumed more than they earned, either demanding wages which increased faster than productivity, or taking advantage of new credit lines, so that personal indebtedness rose more quickly than earnings.[46] This, and its political consequences, had been anticipated by Maude:

> A preoccupation with increasing private consumption is more likely to distort priorities so that public provision lags behind private affluence, as the United States and Australia demonstrate. We ourselves could have better hospitals now, if we wanted them enough.[47]

Similar issues arose with privatization. Clearly conservatives are more comfortable with industry in private hands rather than the state's, but they also prefer competition to monopoly; and some privatizations ended up preserving the very monopolies that, in Thatcher's own analysis, boosted union power,[48] while the pragmatics of government meant that much of the proceeds were simply taken as income to pay for tax cuts, rather than capital to invest in infrastructure.[49]

Conclusion

Margaret Thatcher enjoyed being radical,[50] and did many radical things. As we have seen, conservatism is not necessarily inconsistent with radical change, and indeed many prominent small-c conservatives served Thatcher loyally.[51] However, Thatcher's conservatism (notwithstanding her continuing identification of Burke as her ideological mentor[52]) did not survive into her third term of office. Indeed, many of her actions in the 1980s were ideologically ambiguous.

This is particularly the case with her notorious 'no such thing' statement. Comparison with Angus Maude's formulation of the same basic idea suggests an important purpose behind it – the desire to empower individuals and communities, to give them the space and resources to define and solve their own problems, and to give them a stake in their own future.

Yet, in *The Common Problem*, Maude was careful to point out than there are many meaningful and valuable social structures beyond the bean counters' statistical abstractions. Thatcher, by contrast, used her *Woman's Own* interview to express a hostility to the idea of 'society' which was too vehement for her to acknowledge the value of intermediate institutions. In this respect, while the criticism from the Left was predictable, her views were difficult even for British Conservatives to endorse. As Tocqueville argued, the assumption that *all* we have is men, women and families is as dehumanizing an abstraction as the ones made by the left-wing planners.[53]

NOTES

INTRODUCTION

1. Ewa Atanassow and Alan S. Kahan (eds), *Liberal Moments: Reading Liberal Texts* (London: Bloomsbury, 2017), 1.
2. For a pretty comprehensive indictment of conservatism, see Ted Honderich, *Conservatism: Burke, Nozick, Bush, Blair?* (London: Pluto Press, 2005). For a much more nuanced critique of the conservative attitude to equality, see Peter Dorey, *British Conservatism: The Politics and Philosophy of Inequality* (London: I.B. Tauris, 2011).
3. Daniel Ziblatt, *Conservative Parties and the Birth of Democracy* (Cambridge: Cambridge University Press, 2017).
4. Andrew Gamble, *The Free Economy and the Strong State* (London: Palgrave, 2nd edition, 1994).
5. John Gray, 'The Undoing of Conservatism', in *Enlightenments Wake: Politics and Culture at the Close of the Modern Age* (London: Routledge, 1995), 89–130.
6. For a recent exposition of this view, see Oliver Letwin, *Hearts and Minds: The Battle for the Conservative Party from Thatcher to the Present* (London: Biteback, 2017).
7. The editor's own interpretation of conservative ideology can be found in Mark Garnett, 'Conservatism', in Paul Wetherly (ed), *Political Ideologies* (Oxford: Oxford University Press, 2017), 65–96.

CHAPTER ONE

1. Plato, *The Republic*, trans George Maximillian Anthony Grube (Indianapolis: Hackett, 1974), 562e–563b. Unspecified references are to this edition.
2. *The Analects of Confucius*, trans Arthur Waley (New York: Vintage Books, 1989), 92.
3. Leo Strauss, 'Plato', in Cropsey and Strauss (eds), *History of Political Philosophy* (Chicago: University of Chicago Press, 1987), 34.
4. Plato, *Crito*, in *Five Dialogues: Euthyphro, Apology, Crito, Meno, Phaedo*, trans. George Maximilian Antony Grube and John Cooper, 2nd edition (Indianapolis: Hackett, 2002), 50d, 52a.
5. Plato, *Apology for Socrates*, in *Five Dialogues: Euthyphro, Apology, Crito, Meno, Phaedo*, trans. George Maximilian Antony Grube and John Cooper, 2nd edition (Indianapolis: Hackett, 2002), 41e.

6. Edmund Burke, *Reflections on the Revolution in France*, in Cohen and Fermon (eds), *Princeton Readings in Political Thought* (Princeton: Princeton University Press).

7. Yuval Levin, *The Great Debate: Edmund Burke, Thomas Paine and the Birth of Left and Right* (New York: Basic Books, 2014), 85.

8. Ibid., 86.

9. Michael Oakeshott, 'Rationalism in Politics', in *Rationalism in Politics and Other Essays* (Carmel, IN: Liberty Fund, 1991 edition), 6.

10. Strauss, 'Plato', 62–3.

CHAPTER TWO

1. St Augustine, *The City of God*, trans Marcus Dods (New York: Modern Library, 1993), 493–4.

2. Ibid., 391.

3. St Augustine, 'Letter 1, 2, 22 to Simplician', in *Letters*, Vol. I, trans Wilfrid Parsons (Washington, DC: The Catholic Press University of America, 1951), 205–7.

4. I am using the word 'millennialist' to denote *both* the un-Augustinian, Christian belief that history, with God's guidance, will gradually bring about a worldwide spiritual reformation, *as well as* the belief (of its secular offspring) in the progressive elimination of evil on the planet through the spread of scientific knowledge and 'enlightened' political action.

5. See, for this distinction, *First Corinthians*, 2, 14, in any edition of the New Testament.

6. Thomas Hobbes, *Leviathan* (Oxford: Basil Blackwell, 1946 edn), 308. For sources of these claims in Augustine's writing, see Herbert A. Deane, *The Political and Social Ideas of St. Augustine* (New York: Columbia University Press, 1963), 263, notes 117 and 118.

7. On Augustine's view of participation in just wars, see Deane, *Political and Social Ideas of St. Augustine*, Chapter 5.

8. For more on this theme, see Michael J. Bruno, *Political Augustinianism* (Minneapolis: Fortress), 132.

9. In contrast to Bossuet, Augustine speculates in *The City of God*, BK XVIII, Ch. 47, that before 'Christian times, there were individuals in nations other than the Israelites who were members of the "heavenly city".'

10. Bossuet, Jacques, *Universal History*, trans unknown (London: Samuel Bagster in the Strand, 1810), 155.

11. For development of this theme, see Eric Voegelin, 'On Hegel – A Study in Sorcery', in J. T. Fraser, F. C. Haber and G. H. Muller (eds), *A Study of Time* (Heidelberg: Springer Verlag, 1972), 418–51.

12. To see American millennialism scrupulously documented from New England puritanism to Wilsonian progressivism, see Ernest L. Tuveson, *Redeemer Nation* (Chicago: The University of Chicago Press, 1968).

13. Consider, in this connection, how well received in certain academic quarters are the views of Jürgen Habermas of the neo-Marxist Frankfurt School on 'discursive ethics' and 'ideal speech situations', replacing the old politics of compromise and accommodation with the 'rational pursuit of truth'.

CHAPTER THREE

1. Ibn Khaldun, *The Muqaddimah*, trans F. Rosenthal, ed. N. J. Dawood (Princeton: Princeton University Press, 1967), 111.

2. Ibid., 113.

3. Ibid., 115.

4. See Allen Fromherz, *Ibn Khaldun, Life and Times* (Edinburgh: Edinburgh University Press, 201), 84, for more on Ibn Khaldun's fascinating political role.

5. *The Muqaddimah*, vol. III, 117–18.

6. *The Muqaddimah*, vol. II, 136–7.

7. *The Muqaddimah*, vol. 1, 64.

8. Fromherz, *Ibn Khaldun, Life and Times*, 2–4.

9. Ibid., 4.

CHAPTER FOUR

1. David Hume, *Essays Moral, Political and Literary*, ed. Eugene F. Miller, revised edition (Indianapolis: Liberty Fund, 1987), 40–41.

2. Ibid., 39.

3. Ibid., 40.

4. J. G. A. Pocock, 'Hume and the American Revolution: The Dying Thoughts of a North Briton', in *Virtue, Commerce and History: Essays on Political Thought and History, Chiefly in the Eighteenth Century* (Cambridge: Cambridge University Press, 1985), 125–42, 138. Pocock remarks that 'Hume and [Richard] Price are the two sides of the Tory-radical medal' (140).

5. On Wilkes, see Peter D. G. Thomas, *John Wilkes: A Friend to Liberty* (Clarendon Press: Oxford, 1996). On the politics of the Wilkes and Liberty movement, see John Brewer, *Party Ideology and Popular Politics at the Accession of George III* (Cambridge: Cambridge University Press, 1976), ch. 9.

6. J. Y. T. Greig (ed.), *The Letters of David Hume*, 2 vols. (Oxford: Clarendon Press, 1932), vol. ii, 178.

7. Ibid., 180.

8. Ibid., 197.

9. Giuseppe Giarrizzo, *David Hume Politico e Storico* (Torino: Giulio Einaudi, 1962), esp. Part I, chapter III ('La libertà').

10. Hume, *Essays*, 94.

11. See especially ch. 5 of Duncan Forbes, *Hume's Philosophical Politics* (Cambridge: Cambridge University Press, 1975).

12. David Hume, *A Treatise of Human Nature*, ed. L. A. Selby-Bigge, rev. P. H. Nidditch (Oxford: Clarendon Press, 1978), 566.

13. Hume, *Essays*, 472–3.

14. See Sheldon S. Wolin, 'Hume and Conservatism', *The American Political Science Review*, 48 (1954), 999–1016, 1007–8.

15. Greig (ed.), *Letters of David Hume*, 209.

16. Ibid., 245. There is useful commentary on this passage in G. Birkbeck Hill (ed.), *Letters of David Hume to William Strahan* (Oxford: Clarendon, 1888), 206–10.

17. Greig (ed.), *Letters of David Hume*, 212–13.

18. Ibid., 217–18.

19. David Miller, *Philosophy and Ideology in Hume's Political Thought* (Oxford: Clarendon Press, 1981), 183.

20. H. T. Dickinson, *Liberty and Property: Political Ideology in Eighteenth-Century Britain* (London: Methuen, 1977), ch. 6; Brewer, *Party Ideology and Popular Politics*, ch. 9.

21. Brewer, *Party Ideology and Popular Politics*, 165.

CHAPTER FIVE

1. Leslie G. Mitchell (ed.), *The Writings and Speeches of Edmund Burke*, vol. VIII (Oxford: Clarendon Press, 1989), 138. All parenthetical references are to this edition of the *Reflections*.

2. William Hazlitt, 'Character of Mr Burke, 1807', in Duncan Wu (ed.), *The Selected Writings of William Hazlitt* (London: Pickering & Chatto, 1998), 279.

3. Edmund Burke, *The Speeches of the Right Honourable Edmund Burke* (London: Longman, 1816), vol. III, 47.

4. Mark Philp (ed.), *Rights of Man, Common Sense and Other Political Writings* (Oxford: Oxford University Press), 207–8.

5. Quoted in R. R. Fennessy, *Burke, Paine and the Rights of Man: A Difference of Political Opinion* (The Hague: Martinus Nijhoff, 1963), 194.

6. W. S. Hathaway (ed.), *The Speeches of the Right Honourable William Pitt in the House of Commons* (London: Longman, 1806), vol. IV, 360.

7. See J. J. Sack, 'The Memory of Burke and the Memory of Pitt; English Conservatism Confronts Its Past, 1806–1829', *Historical Journal*, 30.3 (1987), 623–40.

8. See, in particular, *Edmund Burke: The Visionary Who Invented Modern Politics* (London: HarperCollins, 2014) by the Conservative MP Jesse Norman.

CHAPTER SIX

1. Alexander Hamilton, *Federalist 71*, in Terence Ball (ed.), Alexander Hamilton, James Madison and John Jay, *The Federalist*, with *Letters of 'Brutus'*, (Cambridge: Cambridge University Press, 2003), 349.

2. *The Papers of Alexander Hamilton*, ed. Harold C. Syrett and Jacob E. Cooke (27 vols., New York: Columbia University Press, 1961–87), vol. 19, 59–60, hereafter: *PAH*.

3. Hamilton explains the virtues of an energetic executive in *Federalist 70*. His argument for permanence is found in *PAH*, vol. 4, 185.

4. *PAH*, vol. 25, 605.

5. Alexander Hamilton and James Madison, *The Pacificus-Helvidius Debates of 1793–1794*, ed. Morton J. Frisch (Indianapolis: Liberty Fund, 2007), 27.

CHAPTER SEVEN

1. Samuel Taylor Coleridge, *The Friend*, II, ed. Barbara E. Rooke, *Collected Coleridge*, 4 (1969), 201–2.

2. All parenthetical references are to Samuel Taylor Coleridge, *On the Constitution of the Church and State, According to the Idea of Each* (1830), ed. John Colmer, *The Collected Works of Samuel Taylor Coleridge* (*CC*), 10 (Princeton, NJ: Princeton University Press, 1976), 19, 24, 31.

3. Samuel Taylor Coleridge, *Lay Sermons*, ed. R. J. White, *CC*, 6 (1972), 25.

4. Samuel Taylor Coleridge, *Essays on His Times*, I, ed. David. V. Erdman, *CC*, 3 (1977), 32.

5. Ibid., 48–53.

6. Coleridge, *Lay Sermons*, 215 and note.

7. Ibid., 218, 220–1.

8. Earl Leslie Griggs (ed.), *Collected Letters of Samuel Taylor Coleridge*, 6 vols (Oxford: Oxford University Press, 1956–71), II, 806.

9. Coleridge, *Lay Sermons*, 206–7.

10. Ibid., 199.

11. See John Morrow, *Coleridge's Political Thought: Property, Morality and the Limits of Traditional Discourse* (London: Macmillan, 1990), 149–55.

12. Griggs (ed.), *Collected Letters*, IV, 710–11.

13. Morrow, *Coleridge's Political Thought*, 145–6.

14. Ibid., 163–4; J. S. Mill, 'Coleridge', in F. R. Leavis (ed.), *Mill on Bentham and Coleridge* (London: Chatto and Windus, 1965), 155.

CHAPTER EIGHT

1. Leo Strauss, *Liberalism Ancient and Modern* (New York: Basic Books, 1968), v–vii.

2. See, for Strauss's fullest account of this theme, *Persecution and the Art of Writing* (University of Chicago Press, 1952), and, for a more comprehensive elaboration of the historical evidence on its behalf and a classification of its chief forms, Arthur M. Melzer, *Philosophy between the Lines: The Lost History of Esoteric Writing* (University of Chicago Press, 2014).

3. One influential source of this ostensibly damning allegation is Shadia Drury: see her *Leo Strauss and the American Right* (New York: St. Martin's Press, 1997). For the alternative strategy of blaming Strauss's students rather than Strauss himself, see Anne Norton, *Leo Strauss and the Politics of American Empire* (New Haven: Yale University Press, 2004). For responses, see my review of Drury's previous Strauss book, 'Shadia Drury's Critique of Leo Strauss', *The Political Science Reviewer*, 23 (1994), 80–127, and my review of Norton, 'The Ass and the Lion', *Interpretation: A Journal of Political Philosophy*, 32.3 (Summer, 2005), 283–306.

4. Leo Strauss, 'On the Intention of Rousseau', *Social Research*, 14 (1947), 455–87.

5. Leo Strauss, *Natural Right and History* (Chicago: University of Chicago Press, 1953).

6. See Xenophon, *Memorabilia*, 4.4.15; but cf. Richard S. Ruderman, '"Through the Keyhole": Leo Strauss's Rediscovery of Classical Political Philosophy in the 1930s', in Martin Yaffe and Richard Ruderman, eds, *Reorientation: Leo Strauss in the 1930s* (New York: Palgrave Macmillan, 2014), 198–9.

7. Strauss, 'The Three Waves of Modernity', in Hilail Gildin (ed.), *An Introduction to Political Philosophy: Ten Essays by Leo Strauss* (Detroit: Wayne State University Press, 1989), 81–98.

8. Ibid., 94–8.

9. Published in *Interpretation,* 26.3 (Spring, 1999), 353–78.

10. 'Restatement on Xenophon's *Hiero*', in Victor Gourevitch and Michael S. Roth, eds, *On Tyranny*, revised/expanded edition (New York: Free Press, 1991), 194.

11. Strauss, 'Three Waves', 98.

12. 'An Introduction to Heideggerian Existentialism', in *The Rebirth of Classical Political Rationalism: An Introduction to the Thought of Leo Strauss*, ed. Thomas L. Pangle (University of Chicago Press, 1989), 29.

13. To my knowledge, Strauss's most extensive published discussion of contemporary political affairs in the post-war era was his brief discussion of the threat of Communist despotism and the West's response to it in the introduction to his 1964 book *The City and Man* (Chicago: Rand McNally), 4–6, as an instantiation of the crisis of the West he had previously articulated in the introduction to *NRH*. For evidence of Strauss's conservative inclination regarding American politics, see his letter of 18 September 1963 to his long-time correspondent Willmoore Kendall in John Murley and John Alvis, eds, *Willmoore Kendall: Maverick of American Conservatives* (Lanham, MD: Lexington Books, 2002), 247–8.

14. On the original meaning of the term 'liberal' and its transformation into a synonym for 'progressive' beginning in the late nineteenth century, see Daniel B. Klein, 'A Plea Regarding "Liberal"', *Modern Age,* 57.3 (Summer, 2015), 7–16.

15. 'Theses on Feuerbach', XI, in Robert C. Tucker (ed.), *The Marx-Engels Reader,* 2nd ed. (New York: Norton, 1978), 145 (emphasis in original).

16. See Strauss's epilogue to Herbert J. Storing (ed.), *Essays on the Scientific Study of Politics* (New York: Holt, Rinehart, and Winston, 1963), 310, 314–16.

CHAPTER NINE

1. Michael Oakeshott, 'On Being Conservative' (1956), in *Rationalism in Politics and Other Essays* (1962), 188–9.

2. Michael Oakeshott, *The Social and Political Doctrines of Contemporary Europe.* (London: Basic Books, 1940), xxii n.

3. Ibid.

4. Ibid., xx.

5. Ibid., xviii.

6. Ibid., xix.

7. Oakeshott, 'Rationalism in Politics', in *Rationalism in Politics and Other Essays,* 36.

8. On the influence of German thought on Oakeshott see Efraim Podoksik, 'Oakeshott in the Context of German Idealism', in Efraim Podoksik (ed.), *Cambridge Companion to Oakeshott* (Cambridge: Cambridge University Press, 2012), 274–95.

9. Oakeshott, 'The Political Economy of Freedom', in *Rationalism in Politics and Other Essays,* 40–1.

10. Ibid., 38.

11. Ibid., 40.

12. Michael Oakeshott, 'The B.B.C.' [1951], in Luke O'Sullivan (ed.), *The Concept of a Philosophical Jurisprudence: Essays and Reviews 1926–51* (Thorverton: Imprint Academic, 2009), 344.

13. Oakeshott, 'On Being Conservative', in *Rationalism in Politics and Other Essays*, 183.

14. Ibid., 189.

15. Michael Oakeshott, 'The Masses in Representative Democracy', in Albert Hunold (ed.), *Freedom and Serfdom: An Anthology of Western Thought* (Dordrecht: D. Reidel, 19161), 151–170.

CHAPTER TEN

1. Mikhail Katkov, *Moskovskie Vedomosti*, No. 51 (5 March 1864), 1–2.

2. Konstantin Pobedonostev, *Reflections of a Russian Statesman, including the Manifesto on Unshakable Autocracy* (trans. Robert Crozier Long, London: Grant Richards, 1898), 99–100.

3. E. Kholmogorov, 'Russkaia Tsivilizatsiia: Kategorii Ponimaniia', *Tetradi Po Konservatizmu*, ISEPI RAN, No. 3 (2016), 39–63, 57.

4. Edward Thaden, 'The Beginning of Romantic Nationalism in Russia', *American Slavic and East European Review*, 13.4 (December 1954), 509.

5. Edward Thaden, *Conservative Nationalism in Nineteenth-Century Russia* (Seattle: University of Washington Press, 1964), 184–5.

6. Alexandr Dugin, 'Rossiiskaia Identichnist v Sovremennom Mire', Lecture at the Ural Polytechnic University (2012).

7. Boris Mezhuev, 'Suverennoe Bessoznatelnoe', *Tetradi Po Konservatizmu, Tetradi Po Konservatizmu*, ISEPI RAN, No. 3 (2016), 29–38.

8. Ibid.

9. Marc Raeff, 'A Reactionary Liberal: M. N. Katkov', *The Russian Review*, 11.3 (July 1952), 157–67.

10. A. S. Tsipko, 'Liberalnyi Konservatism Nikolaya Berdiaeva i Petra Struve i Zadachi Dekommunizatsii Sovremennoi Rossii', *Tetradi po Konservatizmu*, No. 2 (2014), 31–41.

11. Mikhail Maslin, 'Russkaia Filosofiia v Katolicheskoi Filosofsko-Bogoslovskoi Mysli XX Veka', *Tetradi Po Konservatizmu*, ISEPI RAN, No. 3 (2016), 149–68.

12. Ibid.

CHAPTER ELEVEN

1. Hidetsugu Yagi (2013), *Kenpō Kaisei ga naze hitsuyō ka* [Why Is It Necessary to Revise the Constitution?] (Tokyo: PHP Kenkyūsho) (translation by the present author), 40–2.

2. Christian Winkler, 'The Evolution of the Conservative Mainstream', *Japan Forum*, 24.1 (2012), 51–73.

3. Ibid.; Christian Winkler, 'Between Pork and People: An Analysis of the Policy Balance in the LDP's Election Platforms,' *Journal of East Asian Studies*, 14 (2014), 405–28.

4. See National Diet Library (2004), The Constitution of the Empire of Japan, http://www.ndl.go.jp/constitution/e/etc/c02.html, for an English translation.

5. John Dower, *Embracing Defeat: Japan in the aftermath of World War II* (London: Allen Lane, 1999), 376.

6. Christian Winkler, *The Quest for Japan's New Constitution: An Analysis of Visions and Constitutional Reform Proposals 1980–2009* (Abingdon, Oxon: Routledge, 2011), 52; Abe, Shinzō, *Utsukushii Kuni e* (Towards a Beautiful Nation) (Tokyo: Bungei Shunjū, 2006), 28–9, 122–3.

7. Chaihark Hahm and Sung Ho Kim, *Making We the People: Democratic Constitutional Founding in Postwar Japan and South Korea* (New York: Cambridge University Press, 2015), 130, 201–5.

8. Ibid., 238–9; Kenneth Mori McElwain and Christian G. Winkler, 'What's Unique about the Japanese Constitution? A Comparative and Historical Analysis', *Journal of Japanese Studies*, 41.2 (2015), 249–80.

9. Andrew Gordon, *A History of Modern Japan: From Tokugawa Times to the Present* (New York, Oxford: Oxford University Press, 2003), 61–93.

10. Yatsuhiro Nakagawa, Hidetsu Yagi and Shōichi Watanabe, 'Edmund Burke ni manabu Hoshu shugi no Daidō' [The Great Principles of Conservatism as learned from Edmund Burke], *Shokun,*8 (2000), 84.

11. Christian Winkler, 'Consistent Conservatism in Changing Times: An Analysis of Japanese Conservative Intellectuals' Thought', *Social Science Japan Journal*, 15.1 (2012), 103.

12. Jun Etō, Nihon yo, horobiru no ka [Oh Japan, Are You Going to Perish?] (Tokyo: Bungei Shunjū, 1994), 47.

13. Winkler, 'Consistent Conservatism', 105.

14. Roger Scruton, *The Meaning of Conservatism* (Basingstoke and New York: Palgrave MacMillan, 2001), 38–9.

15. Ibid.

16. Iain Hampsher-Monk (ed.), *Edmund Burke: Revolutionary Writings* (Cambridge: Cambridge University Press, 2014), 37.

17. Michael Oakeshott, *Rationalism in Politics and Other Essays* (London: Methuen, 1962), 27.

18. Hidetsugu Yagi, 'Haka kara no Tōchi arui ha Shisha no Minshushugi' [Rule from the Grave or Democracy of the Dead], *Hatsugensha*, 72, (2000), 38.

19. Translated in Winkler, *Japan's New Constitution*, 115.

20. Fujiwara Masahiko and Giles Murray, *Kokka no Hinkaku: The Dignity of the Nation* (Tokyo: IBC Publishing, 2007), 121.

21. See McElwain and Winkler, 'What's Unique about the Japanese Constitution?'

22. Glenn D. Hook and Gavan McCormack, *Japan's Contested Constitution: Documents and Analysis* (London and New York: Routledge, 2001), 191–2.

23. Hidesugu Yagi, *Nihonkoku Kenpô to ha nani ka* [What is the Japanese Constitution?] (Tokyo: PHP Shinsho, 2003), 214–16.

24. Kanji Nishio, *Kojin shugi to ha nani ka* (What Is Individualism?) (Tokyo: PHP Kenkyūsho, 2007), 17, 30.

25. Hidetsugu Yagi (1996), 'Fūfu bessei ha Shakai wo hakkai suru', *Shokun*, 3 (1996), 214–222.

26. For a discussion on various conservative proposals, see, for example, Winkler, *Japan's New Constitution*, 161–5.

27. Robert Nisbet, *Conservatism: Dream and Reality* (New Brunswick and London: Transaction Publishers, 2008 ed.), 115.

28. Quoted in George Panichas, *The Essential Russell Kirk: Selected Essays*. (Wilmington: ISI Books, 2007), 19–20.

29. See, for example, Takeshi Nakajima, 'Shisō to Monogatari wo ushinatta Hoshu to Uyoku: '"Kaiken-Moe" "Yasukuni-moe" Danpentekina Nekkyō wo koeyo' (Conservatives and Right-Wing Activists Who Have Forgotten Their Ideas and Lore: Overcome the Fragmentary Frenzy of the Infatuation with Constitutional Reform, Yasukuni), *Ronza*, 146 (2007), 47–54; and Winkler, 'Consistent Conservatism'.

CHAPTER TWELVE

1. Ludwig Erhard, *Prosperity through Competition* (New York: Frederick A Prager, 1958), 2–3.

2. Paolo Pombeni, 'The ideology of Christian Democracy', *Journal of Political Ideologies*, 5.3 (2000), 289–300, focuses on the influence of Catholic thinkers. For general surveys see Geoffrey Pridham, *Christian Democracy in Western Europe* (London: Routledge, 1979); and David Hanley (ed.), *Christian Democracy in Europe: A Comparitive Perspective* (London: Continuum, 1994). Christian Democracy has also been influential in South America (especially Chile and Brazil), but this article focuses on Europe where the tradition has been most prominent.

3. Wolfram Kaiser, 'Christian Democracy in Twentieth-century Europe', *Journal of Contemporary History*, 39.1 (January 2004), 127–35.

4. Erhard, *Prosperity*, 102–3.

5. Alfred C. Mierzejewski, *Ludwig Erhard: A Biography* (University of North Carolina Press, 2004), 184.

6. See Arthur Olsen, '"Gauliist" Adenaeur Challenges Erhard', *New York Times*, 26 (July 1964), http://www.nytimes.com/1964/07/26/gaullist-adenauer-challenges-erhard.html.

7. Quoted in Arthur Schlesinger, *A Thousand Days: John F Kennedy in the White House* (Boston: Houghton Mifflin, 1965), 291.

8. For 'catch-all' parties, see especially Otto Kirchheimer (1966), 'The Transformation of Western European Party Systems', in Joseph La Polambara

and M. Weiner (eds), *Political Parties and Political Development* (New Jersey: Princeton University Press).

9. Jan-Werner Muller, '1968 as Event, Millieu, and Ideology', in Jan-Werner Muller (ed.), *German Ideologies since 1945* (Houndmills: Palgrave Macmillan, 2003), 125.

10. Jan-Werner Muller, 'The End of Christian Democracy', *Foreign Affairs*, 15 July, 2014.

CHAPTER THIRTEEN

1. *Political Vision of AKP Parti (Justice and Development Party) 2023: Politics, Society and the World*, 2012. https://www.akparti.org.tr/english/akparti/2023-political-vision, 4, 5, 8.

2. Michael M. Gunter, 'Erdogan and the Decline of Turkey', *Middle East Policy*, 23.4 (Winter 2016), 123.

3. Ergün Ozbudun, 'From political Islam to Conservative Democracy: The Case of the Justice and Development Party in Turkey', *South European Society & Politics*, (2006), 543–57.

4. Quoted in Andrew Mango, *Ataturk* (London: John Murray, 1999), 463.

5. Gareth Jenkins, 'Muslim Democrats in Turkey?', *Survival*, 45.1 (2003), 45–66.

6. See David Fromkin, *A Peace to End All Peace: The Fall of the Ottoman Empire and the Creation of the Modern Middle East* (New York: Henry Holt, 1989).

7. Leslie G. Mitchell (ed.), *The Writings and Speeches of Edmund Burke* (Oxford: Clarendon Press, 1989), vol. VIII, 142.

8. Nilüfer Göle, 'Secularism and Islamism in Turkey: The Making of Elites and Counter-elites', *The Middle East Journal*, 51.1 (1997), 46–58.

9. Findings published by Ipsos-Mori in 2016; https://www.ipsosglobaltrends.com/wp-content/uploads/2017/04/Slide13-6.jpg

10. Ziya Önis, 'Monopolising the Centre: The AKP and the Uncertain Path of Turkish Democracy', *The International Spectator,* 50.2 (2015), 22–41.

11. Berk Esen and Sebnem Gumuscu, 'Rising Competitive Authoritarianism in Turkey', *Third World Quarterly*, 37.9 (2016), 1581–1606.

12. Burak Bekdil, 'Turkey's Slide into Authoritarianism', *Middle East Quarterly*, 24.1 (2017), 1–9.

13. Ibid.

14. See Simon Mabon, 'Sovereignty, Bare Life and the Arab Uprisings', *Third World Quarterly* (2017) and *Saudi Arabia and Iran: Power and Rivalry in the Middle East* (London: I.B. Tauris, 2015).

15. Omer Taspinar, 'Turkey: The New Model?', in Robin Wright (ed.), *The Islamists Are Coming: Who They Really Are* (Washington, DC: Wilson Center and the U.S. Institute of Peace, 2012), 1–11.

16. Halil Karaveli, 'Erdogan's Journey: Conservatism and Authoritarianism in Turkey', *Foreign Affairs* (November/December 2016), 121–30.

CHAPTER FOURTEEN

1. Charles de Gaulle, War Memoirs: Volume One, The Call to Honour, 1940-1942 (London: Collins, 1955), 1.

2. Maurice Aghulon, *De Gaulle: Histoire, Symbole, Mythe* (Paris: Plon, 2000).

3. The locus classicus is Jean Lacouture, *De Gaulle the Rebel :1890–1944* (New York: W. W. Norton, 1990).

4. Marc Sadoun, Jean-François Sirinelli and Robert Vandenbussche (eds), *La politique sociale du Général de Gaulle* (Villneuve d'Ascq: Centre d'histoire de la région du nord, 1989), 45–6.

5. Charles de Gaulle, *War Memoirs* (London: Collins, 1955); Aghulon, *De Gaulle*, Ch. 4.

6. Alistair Horne, *A Savage War of Peace: Algeria 1954–1962* (London: Macmillan, 1977), Ch. 12.

7. René Rémond, *The Right in France* (Philadelphia: University of Pennsylvania Press, Philadelphia, 1966).

8. Ibid.

9. Seen in Pierre Viansson-Ponté, *The King and His Court* (Boston: Houghton Mifflin, Boston, 1964), in which de Gaulle's entourage is guyed as a monarchy.

10. Douglas Johnson, 'The Political Principles of General de Gaulle', *International Affairs,* 45 (1965), 650–62.

11. Gaullism is placed in this category by both Daniel Seiler and Klaus Von Beyme, *Political Parties in Western Democracies* (Aldershot: Gower, 1985). On social composition see Jean Charlot, *The Gaullist Phenomenon* (London: Unwin, 1970).

12. Philip M. Williams, *The French Parliament 1958–67* (London: Unwin, 1968), 85–9.

13. Wolf Mendl, *Deterrence and Persuasion* (London: Faber, 1970), and Wilfred Kohl (1971), *French Nuclear Diplomacy (Princeton, NJ: Princeton University Press)*.

14. Nora Beloff, *The General says 'no'* (Harmondsworth: Penguin, 1963).

15. John Newhouse, *Collision in Brussels* (London: Faber, 1967).

16. Jean-Baptiste Duroselle, 'General de Gaulle's Europe and Jean Monnet's Europe', *The World Today,* 22 (1966), 1–13.

17. Michèle Cointet, *De Gaulle et l'Algérie française* (Paris: Perin, 2012) Epilogue.

18. Raymond Aron, *The Great Debate* (New York: Doubleday, 1965) Ch. 4.

19. Speech by de Gaulle, Casablanca, 8 August 1943.

CHAPTER FIFTEEN

1. Full text available at http://www.presidency.ucsb.edu/ws/?pid=43130.

2. For the 1966 governor's race, see Matthew Dallek, *The Right Moment: Ronald Reagan's First Victory and the Decisive Turning Point in American Politics*

(New York: Free Press, 2000); Donald T. Critchlow, *When Hollywood Was Right* (Cambridge: Cambridge University Press, 2013), 184–215; Lou Cannon, *Governor Reagan: His Rise to Power* (New York: Public Affairs, 2003), 133–48; Totton J. Anderson and Eugene C. Lee, 'The 1966 Election in California', *Western Political Quarterly*, 20.2 (June 1967), 535–54; Kurt Shuperra, *Triumph of the Right: The Rise of the California Conservative Movement, 1945–66* (London: Routledge, 1998), 205–11.

3. Cannon, *Governor Reagan,* 186.

4. Ibid., 194.

5. Quoted in ibid., 352–53.

6. The issue of reproductive rights in the Reagan presidency is discussed in Donald T. Critchlow, *Intended Consequences: Birth Control, Abortion, and the Federal Government in Modern America* (Oxford: Oxford University Press, 1999); and Mary Ziegler, *After Roe: The Lost History of the Abortion Debate* (Harvard: Harvard University Press, 2015).

7. The literature on Ronald Reagan is immense, including studies of his movie career, governorship, election campaigns, presidency and policies. The view that the 'Reagan Revolution' failed was first articulated by David Stockman, who served a Director of Office of Management and Budget under Reagan, 1981–85, in *The Triumph of Politics: Why the Reagan Revolution Failed* (New York: Harper & Row, 1986). The theme of a failed revolution is explained in Larry M. Schwab, *The Illusion of a Conservative Reagan Revolution* (New York: Routledge, 2016). Historians Julian Zelizer and Meg Jacobs suggest a failed conservative revolution in their co-authored volume *Conservatives in Power: The Reagan Years, 1981–89* (Boston: Bedford, 2013). Interpretations for the success of Reagan's agenda can be found in Martin Anderson, *Revolution* (New York: Harcourt, 1988) and Steven F. Haywood, *The Age of Reagan: The Conservative Counter Revolution, 1980–1989* (New York: Crown Forum, 2009). A good summary of Reagan, the skilled politician and principled pragmatist is found in Donald T. Critchlow, *Republican Character: From Nixon to Reagan* (Philadelphia: University of Pennsylvania Press, 2017). The best biography of Reagan is Iwan Morgan, *Reagan: An American Icon* (London: I.B. Tauris, 2016).

8. 'Reagan Blames "Iron Triangle" for Nation's Ills', *Los Angeles Times* (December 14, 1988).

CHAPTER SIXTEEN

1. The transcript of the full interview is available on the Margaret Thatcher Foundation website, at http://www.margaretthatcher.org/document/106689. The journalist, Douglas Keay, slightly rewrote Thatcher's words, but no one has claimed that Keay misrepresented or misinterpreted her intended meaning.

2. Vernon Bogdanor, 'From an Ism to a Wasm', *Times Higher Education Supplement* (7 May 2004), https://www.timeshighereducation.com/books/from-an-ism-to-a-wasm/188530.article.

3. Margaret Thatcher, *The Downing Street Years 1979–1990* (London: HarperCollins, 1993), 626.

4. https://www.theguardian.com/politics/2005/oct/04/conservatives2005. conservatives3.

5. Not actually written by Thatcher, but, like her speeches and manifestos, extensively honed by her.

6. For example, *Downing Street Years*, 140–1, 336, 571.

7. Ibid., 14.

8. For example, David Cannadine, *Margaret Thatcher: A Life and Legacy* (Oxford: Oxford University Press, 2017), 113.

9. Margaret Thatcher, *The Path to Power* (London: HarperCollins, 1995).

10. Charles Moore, *Margaret Thatcher: The Authorized Biography, Volume One: Not for Turning* (London: Allen Lane, 2013), 192–3.

11. Mark Garnett and Kevin Hickson, *Conservative Thinkers: The Key Contributors to the Political Thought of the Conservative Party* (Manchester: Manchester University Press, 2009).

12. Andrew Denham and Mark Garnett, *Keith Joseph* (London: Acumen, 2002), 250–3.

13. Thatcher, *Downing Street Years*, 130.

14. Ibid., 126.

15. Cf. Oliver Letwin, *Hearts and Minds: The Battle for the Conservative Party from Thatcher to the Present* (London: Biteback Publishing, 2017), 51–4.

16. Thatcher, *Downing Street Years*, 712.

17. Despite Hayek's own clear statement that he was *not* a conservative. See his 'Why I Am Not a Conservative', in *The Constitution of Liberty*, 395–411 (London: Routledge & Kegan Paul, 1960).

18. Geoffrey Brennan and Alan Hamlin, 'Comprehending Conservatism: Frameworks and Analysis', *Journal of Political Ideologies*, 19.2 (2014), 227–39; Kieron O'Hara, 'Conservatism, Epistemology and Value', *The Monist*, 99 (2016), 423–40.

19. Mark Garnett, *From Anger to Apathy* (London: Jonathan Cape, 2007); Dominic Sandbrook, *Seasons in the Sun: The Battle for Britain, 1974–1979* (London: Allen Lane, 2012).

20. Thatcher, *Downing Street Years*, 5, 15, 19, 38.

21. Ibid., 173, 235, 791, 264, 743.

22. Edmund Burke, *Reflections on the Revolution in France* (Harmondsworth: Penguin, 1968 edn), 172; cf. *Downing Street Years*, 638.

23. Thatcher, *Downing Street Years*, 285.

24. Ibid., 618, 568–9.

25. Michael Oakeshott. 'On Being Conservative', in *Rationalism in Politics and Other Essays* (Indianapolis: Liberty Fund, 1991 edn), 412.

26. Kieron O'Hara, 'The Conservative Dialectic of Margaret Thatcher's First Term', in B. W. Hart and R. Carr (eds), *The Foundations of the British Conservative Party* (London: Continuum, 2013), 39–61.

27. Thatcher, *Downing Street Years*, 6–7, 13, 28, 104.

28. Ibid., 144–6, 800.

29. Ibid., 105 (and cf. 103), 143, 780.

30. Ibid., 14 (and cf. 100), 272–3.

31. Ibid., 678ff.

32. Cannadine, *Margaret Thatcher*, 81.

33. Thatcher, *Downing Street Years*, 279, 590–3, 606, 608, 614.

34. Ibid., 688–690. Cf. Denham and Garnett, *Keith Joseph*, 418.

35. Cf. Denham and Garnett, *Keith Joseph*, 219–25; Letwin, *Hearts and Minds*, 64–8.

36. Charles Moore, *Margaret Thatcher: The Authorized Biography, Volume Two: Everything She Wants* (London: Allen Lane, 2015), 33.

37. Garnett and Hickson, *Conservative Thinkers* (Chapter 5).

38. Angus Maude, *The Common Problem: A Policy for the Future* (London: Constable, 1969), 45.

39. Ibid., 42.

40. Ibid., 41. Note how Maude enclosed the word 'society' in quote marks. His criticism is not of the notion of society in itself, but rather a construct he considered artificial.

41. Thatcher, *Downing Street Years*, 29.

42. Maude, *Common Problem*, 16, 50.

43. For example, *Downing Street Years*, 146, 279, 601, 618, 625 ff.

44. Maude, *Common Problem*, 25, cf. 51.

45. http://www.margaretthatcher.org/document/106689

46. Cannadine, *Margaret Thatcher*, 83.

47. Maude, *Common Problem*, 113.

48. Thatcher, *Downing Street Years*, 101–2.

49. Cannadine, *Margaret Thatcher*, 82.

50. For example, *Downing Street Years*, 264, 308, 565, 579, 605.

51. O'Hara, 'Conservative Dialectic'.

52. Thatcher, *Downing Street Years*, 753.

53. Alexis de Tocqueville (2003), *Democracy in America* (London: Penguin, 2003 edn), 805–6.

FURTHER READING

CHAPTER 1

Oakeshott, Michael. 'Rationalism in Politics'. In *Rationalism in Politics and Other Essays* (Carmel, IN: Liberty Fund, 1991).

Plato. *Five Dialogues*, trans. George Maximilian Antony Grube (Indianapolis, IN: Hackett Publishing, 1981).

Plato. *Republic*, trans. George Maximilian Antony Grube (Indianapolis, IN: Hackett Publishing, 1974).

Strauss, Leo. 'Plato'. In Cropsey and Strauss (eds), *History of Political Philosophy* (Chicago: University of Chicago Press, 1987).

CHAPTER 2

Bruno, Michael J. *Political Augustinianism* (Minneapolis: Fortress Press, 2014). Competent summaries of major twentieth-century and contemporary Augustinian scholarship.

Cochrane, Charles N. *Christianity and Classical Culture* (Oxford: Oxford University Press, 1944). Classic work with over one hundred pages on Augustine's theory of the human personality, bridging the gap between spirit and matter in both classical idealism and classical materialism.

CHAPTER 3

Dale, Stephen. *The Orange Trees of Marrakech: Ibn Khaldun and the Science of Man* (Cambridge, MA: Harvard University Press, 2015).

Fischel, Walter. *Ibn Khaldun and Tamerlane* (Oakland: University of California Press, 1952).

Fromherz, Allen. *Ibn Khaldun: Life and Times* (Edinburgh: Edinburgh University Press, 2011).

Ibn Khaldun. *The Muqaddimah, An Introduction to History*, 3 vols, trans. Franz Rosenthal (Princeton, NJ: Princeton University Press, 1967).

Mahdi, Muhsin. *Ibn Khaldun's Philosophy of History* (Chicago, IL: University of Chicago Press, 1971).

CHAPTER 4

Forbes, Duncan. *Hume's Philosophical Politics* (Cambridge: Cambridge University Press, 1975).

Forbes, Duncan. 'Politics and History in Hume', *Historical Journal*, 6 (1963): 280–95.

Harris, James A. *Hume: An Intellectual Biography* (Cambridge: Cambridge University Press, 2015).

Livingston, Donald. *Philosophical Melancholy and Delirium: Hume's Pathology of Philosophy* (Chicago: University of Chicago Press, 1998).

Miller, David. *Philosophy and Ideology in Hume's Political Thought* (Oxford: Clarendon Press, 1981).

Wolin, Sheldon. Hume and Conservatism, *The American Political Science Review*, 48 (1954): 999–1016.

CHAPTER 5

Bourke, Richard. *Empire and Revolution: The Political Life of Edmund Burke* (Princeton: Princeton University Press, 2015).

Burke, Edmund. *The Writings and Speeches of Edmund Burke* (Oxford: Oxford University Press, published in nine volumes between 1981 and 2015, under the general editorship of Paul Langford).

Dwan, David and Christopher Insole. *The Cambridge Companion to Edmund Burke* (Cambridge: Cambridge University Press, 2012).

Lock, F. P. *Edmund Burke* (Oxford: Oxford University Press, published in two volumes in 1998 and 2006).

CHAPTER 6

Brookhiser, Richard. *Alexander Hamilton, American* (New York: Free Press, 1999).

Chernow, Ron. *Alexander Hamilton* (New York: Penguin, 2004).

Federici, Michael P. *The Political Philosophy of Alexander Hamilton* (Baltimore: Johns Hopkins University Press, 2012).

Knott, Stephen F. *Alexander Hamilton and the Persistence of Myth* (Lawrence: University Press of Kansas, 2002).

McDonald, Forrest. *Alexander Hamilton: A Biography* (New York and London: W.W. Norton, 1982).

Rossiter, Clinton. *Alexander Hamilton and the Constitution* (New York: Harcourt, Brace & World, 1964).

CHAPTER 7

Allen, Peter, S. T. 'Coleridge's *Church and State* and the Idea of an Intellectual Establishment', *Journal of the History of Ideas*, 46.1 (1985): 89–106.

Calleo, David. *Coleridge and the Idea of the Modern State* (New Haven, CT: Yale University Press, 1966).

Coleman, Deidre. *Coleridge and 'The Friend' (1809–10)* (Oxford: Oxford University Press, 1988).

Colmer, John. *Coleridge, Critic of Society* (Oxford: Oxford University Press, 1959).

Edwards, Pamela. 'Coleridge on Politics and Religion'. In Frederick Burwick (ed.), *The Oxford Handbook of Samuel Taylor Coleridge* (Oxford: Oxford University Press, 2012).

Leask, Nigel. *The Politics of Imagination in Coleridge's Political Thought* (London: Macmillan, 1988).

Morrow, John (ed.). *Coleridge's Writings, Volume 1: On Politics and Society* (Princeton: Princeton University Press, 1989).

CHAPTER 8

Gildin, Hilail (ed.). *An Introduction to Political Philosophy: Ten Essays by Leo Strauss* (Detroit: Wayne State University Press, 1989).

Pangle, Thomas. *Leo Strauss: An Introduction to His Thought and Intellectual Legacy* (Baltimore: Johns Hopkins University Press, 2006).

Strauss, Leo. *Natural Right and History* (Chicago: University of Chicago Press, 1953).

Strauss, Leo. *What Is Political Philosophy? And Other Studies* (Glencoe, IL: Free Press, 1959).

Zuckert, Michael P. and Catherine H. Zuckert. *Leo Strauss and the Problem of Political Philosophy* (Chicago: University of Chicago Press, 2014).

CHAPTER 9

Franco, Paul and Leslie Marsh (eds). *A Companion to Michael Oakeshott* (Pennsylvania, PA: Penn State University Press, 2012).

Oakeshott, Michael. *Lectures in the History of Political Thought* (Thorverton, UK: Imprint Academic, 2006).

Oakeshott, Michael. *On Human Conduct* (Oxford: Oxford University Press, 1975).

Oakeshott, Michael. *Rationalism in Politics and Other Essays* (London: Methuen, 1962).

Podoksik, Efraim (ed.). *The Cambridge Companion to Oakeshott* (Cambridge: Cambridge University Press, 2012).

CHAPTER 10

Berlin, Isaiah. *Russian Thinkers* (London: Penguin, 1994).

Conroy, Mary. *Emerging Democracy in Late Imperial Russia. Case Studies on Local Self-Government, State Duma Elections, the Tsarist Government, and the*

State Council before and during World War I (Niwot: University of Colorado Press, 1998).

Kelly, Aileen. *Views from the Other Shore. Essays on Herzen, Chekhov, and Bakhtin* (New Haven, CT: Yale University Press, 1999).

Lossky, Nikolay. *History of Russian Philosophy* (London: George Allen and Unwin, 1952).

Walicki, Andrzej. *A History of Russian Thought. From the Enlightenment to Marxism* (Stanford: Stanford University Press, 1979).

CHAPTER 11

Winkler, Christian. *The Quest for Japan's New Constitution: An Analysis of Visions and Constitutional Reform Proposals, 1980–2009* (Abingdon, UK: Routledge, 2011).

Winkler, Christian G. 'The Evolution of the Conservative Mainstream', *Japan Forum* 24.1 (2012): 51–73.

Winkler, Christian G. 'Consistent Conservatism in Changing Times: An Analysis of Japanese Conservative Intellectuals' Thought', *Social Science Japan Journal*, 15.1 (2012): 93–110.

CHAPTER 12

Hanley, David. (ed.). *Christian Democracy in Europe: A Comparative Perspective* (London: Continuum, 1994).

Nicholls, Anthony James. *Freedom with Responsibility: The Social Market Economy in Germany, 1918–1963* (Oxford: Clarendon, 1994).

Pridham, Geofrrey. *Christian Democracy in Western Germany: The CDU/CSU in Government and Opposition, 1945–1976* (London: Croom Helm, 1977).

CHAPTER 13

Fromkin, David. *A Peace to End All Peace: The Fall of the Ottoman Empire and the Creation of the Modern Middle East* (New York: Henry Holt, 1989).

Karaveli, Halil. Erdogan's Journey: Conservatism and Authoritarianism in Turkey, *Foreign Affairs* (November/December 2016): 121–30.

Mango, Andrew. *Attaturk* (London: John Murray, 1999).

Ozbudun, Ergun. From Political Islam to Conservative Democracy: The Case of the Justice and Development Party in Turkey, *South European Society & Politics*, 11 (2006): 543–57.

CHAPTER 14

Charlot, Jean. *The Gaullist Phenomenon* (London: Unwin, 1970).

Hoffmann, Stanley. *De Gaulle in Decline or Renewal? France since the 1930s* (New York: Viking, 1974).

Hoffmann, Stanley and Inge. The Will to Grandeur: de Gaulle as Political Artist, *Daedalus,* 97 (1968): 829–97.

Rémond, René. *The Right in France* (Philadelphia: University of Pennsylvania Press, 1966).

Tenzer, Nicolas. *La Face cachée du gaullisme* (Paris: Hachette, 1998).

CHAPTER 15

Critchlow, Donald. *Republican Character: From Nixon to Reagan* (Philadelphia, PA: University of Philadelphia Press, 2017).

Critchlow, Donald. *When Hollywood Was Right* (Cambridge: Cambridge University Press, 2013).

Morgan, Iwan. *Reagan: An American Icon* (London: I.B. Tauris, 2016).

Zelizer, Julian and Meg Jacobs. *Conservatives in Power: The Reagan Years, 1981–89* (Boston, MA: Bedford, 2013).

CHAPTER 16

Cannadine, David. *Margaret Thatcher: A Life and Legacy* (Oxford: Oxford University Press, 2017).

Gilmour, Ian. *Dancing with Dogma: Britain under Thatcherism* (London: Simon & Schuster, 1992).

Lawson, Nigel. *The View from No. 11: Memoirs of a Tory Radical* (London: Bantam Press, 1992).

O'Hara, Kieron. 'The Conservative Dialectic of Margaret Thatcher's First Term'. In Bradley W. Hart and Richard Carr (eds), *The Foundations of the British Conservative Party* (London: Continuum, 2013), 39–61.

Thatcher, Margaret. *The Downing Street Years 1979–1990* (London: HarperCollins, 1993).

INDEX

www.ingramcontent.com/pod-product-compliance
Lightning Source LLC
Chambersburg PA
CBHW062032270326
41929CB00014B/2409